Fig. 1 Hotel Clou and the Wino store in Mauerstrasse 15. The picture was taken on 17 February 1950. A good 40 years later it hosted Elektro, Berlin's smallest Techno club

THE FIRST DAYS OF BERLIN

THE FIRST DAYS OF BERLIN

The Sound of Change

Ulrich Gutmair

Translated by Simon Pare

polity

Originally published in German as *Die ersten Tage von Berlin. Der Sound der Wende* © 2013 Klett-Cotta - J.G. Cotta'sche Buchhandlung Nachfolger GmbH, Stuttgart. English edition published by arrangement with Michael Gaeb Literary Agency

This English edition © Polity Press, 2021

The translation of this work was supported by a grant from the Goethe-Institut

Polity Press
65 Bridge Street
Cambridge CB2 1UR, UK

Polity Press
101 Station Landing
Suite 300
Medford, MA 02155, USA

ISBN-13: 978-1-5095-4729-6
ISBN-13: 978-1-5095-4730-2 (paperback)

A catalogue record for this book is available from the British Library.

Library of Congress Control Number: 2021938641

Typeset in 10.75pt on 14pt Janson by
Cheshire Typesetting Ltd, Cuddington, Cheshire
Printed and bound in Great Britain by TJ Books Ltd, Padstow, Cornwall

The publisher has used its best endeavours to ensure that the URLs for external websites referred to in this book are correct and active at the time of going to press. However, the publisher has no responsibility for the websites and can make no guarantee that a site will remain live or that the content is or will remain appropriate.

Every effort has been made to trace all copyright holders, but if any have been overlooked the publisher will be pleased to include any necessary credits in any subsequent reprint or edition.

For further information on Polity, visit our website:
politybooks.com

For Tal and Amalia

Contents

Illustrations

Acknowledgements

My heartfelt thanks to everyone who told me their stories and also to those who contributed their memories but were not named in the text: Bettina Ellerkamp, Florian Zeyfang, Jörg Heitmann and Jutta Kunde.

I also owe a debt of gratitude to Alexandra Corell, Annette Maechtel, Gabriele, Hannelore and Werner Gutmair, Henriette Gallus, Martin Hossbach, Maximilian Dorner, Micz Flor, Ronald Düker, Silvan Linden and the folks from Sourcefabric.

Preface to the English Edition

Some thirty years ago, Berlin was a sleepy place, detached from the rest of the world. Long gone were the days when the city was the most powerful industrial centre in continental Europe; a metropolis, birthplace of artistic avant-gardes, battleground for political ideas, welcoming place for revolutionaries of all kinds. The Nazis had exiled most of the artists, many of whom were Jewish, who had made Berlin a vibrant, hypermodern city. They had considered jazz to be 'un-German', and modern art to be 'degenerate'.

On 2 May 1945, the Red Army finally conquered Berlin. The tyranny that caused the death of 50 million people in Europe, and was supported by some Germans until the bitter end, was over. The Cold War split the city into two halves. As a whole, Berlin found itself pushed from the centre of German culture to the periphery. What remained was the myth of those Golden Years.

The eastern part of the city came under Soviet administration. The socialist German Democratic Republic was founded and East Berlin became its capital. In 1961, the Wall was built to prevent East Germans from fleeing to the West. In the wake of the 1980s, this socialist state was broke and, ironically, kept alive for some more years through loans from West Germany. But the GDR was not able to reform itself. Its government was finally brought down by a peaceful revolution of its citizens. Similar revolutions took place in most of the countries in Eastern Europe, showing the world that people really have the power – if the ones in charge decide not to use rifles and tanks against them. On 4 June 1989, the Chinese government brutally crushed the democratic movement in Tiananmen Square. So when hundreds of thousands began to join the anti-government demonstrations in Berlin and Leipzig in the autumn of the same year, the fear that the East German Politburo would opt for the 'Chinese solution' was in the air.

After 1945 the Western part of Berlin was controlled by the Western Allies – the USA, the UK and France – and later became a part of the Federal Republic of Germany in the West. During the Cold War, the Western Allies considered West Berlin to be 'the showcase of the Free World' within the Eastern Bloc. Surrounded by the Wall, the enclave relied on subsidies from the West German government. Had it not been for the student revolt in 1967, the squatters' movement, the young Germans who came here to avoid the draft, and artists like Einstürzende Neubauten, Iggy Pop and David Bowie, who loved the morbid charm of this grey and forgotten place, we would not have been able to say that anything significant happened here during the 1970s and 1980s.

When the Wall was opened by East German government officials, on the evening of 9 November 1989, the city slowly woke up again. The first days of reunified Berlin began.

This is a book about memory. When I started writing it, about fifteen years ago, I wanted to deliver a historical account of a short but formative transition period. In the year between the fall of the Wall and the reunification of the two states, a space of possibility had opened up. While many of the elder East Berliners were struggling to adapt to the new system, young people from Berlin and from all over the world had the economic and political freedom to realize their dreams, to create artworks and situations in a communal spirit. Houses were squatted, galleries were opened, basements were turned into clubs.

I had moved to Berlin from Bavaria to study history three weeks before the Wall fell. Now, I could study history in the making. I began to understand how revolutionary events actually disrupt and transcend its course. In those days, even the passage of time felt out of control. It seemed to speed up. Every day a new experience, every night a new sound. Rapid political change was followed by a fast transformation of city space. And paradoxically, it also seemed as though time stood still. Berlin-Mitte was an almost pastoral cityscape, a utopia in the true sense of the word. A non-place, in which the sound of the bass drum would set things in motion.

When we went out for a night of dancing in some makeshift club, sometimes we would reach a state of euphoria that, by definition, is the closest a living being can get to the eternal. Forgetting the past and the future, while getting lost in music, we would enter the magical time-space of absolute presence.

When I started to write this book and tried to fill the gaps in my memory, to reclaim my own history that did not find many references in the rapidly changing surroundings, I studied newspapers and books, and more significantly, I asked a variety of people to tell me their stories. This book is also their book, and I have tried to treat all those stories with respect while keeping the somewhat cruel distance you need to write truthfully.

I expected all the popular clubs, like Tresor or E-Werk, to be remembered, and eminent figures in the art and music scene to get the recognition they deserved. So I saw it as my duty to try and catch the ephemeral, to detect the zeitgeist in the lives of those who might be overlooked even though their presence and work were important in forming the culture of this temporary autonomous zone that shapes the image of Berlin to this day.

While working on this book, I spent considerable time trying to find ways to avoid writing 'I', thinking that there is a pompousness in it – if not accredited by necessity, the economy of the text itself. But this 'I' contained a higher truth. This is a history of the events and developments in Berlin-Mitte that tries to take into account as many perspectives as possible. But ultimately, it is also my personal story.

This is a book about cities. What Berliners fear most today is that their city might meet the fate of London, Paris and New York, where only the wealthy can afford to live, or even worse, where many buildings are not places to dwell in any more, but mere investments, staying empty for most of the year.

After Berlin had again become the capital of Germany, for some time its population rose by about 50,000 per year. At the same time, city government had to sell many of the publicly owned housing enterprises to fill empty coffers. When, after the global financial crisis in 2008, capital was fleeing into real estate, investors from all over the world discovered that real estate was relatively cheap in Berlin.

Berlin has seen a steep rise in rents in recent years – and Berlin is traditionally a city of renters, not owners. So in 2020, R2G – the coalition of Social Democrats, Socialists and the Green Party governing Berlin – decided to introduce legislation to freeze rents. Even though Germany's Federal Constitution Court has declared the Berlin rent freeze to be null and void in the meantime, it is hailed by progressives as a powerful tool for the whole of Germany in order to keep cities diverse places, inhabitable for the many, not only the few.

For cities to be places open for everyone, culture has to play an important role. In May 2021, the German parliament decided that nightclubs should legally cease to be considered as places for entertainment and would now be treated as cultural sites. It means that urban planning regulations and building laws concerning museums and theatres now also apply to clubs. This is good news. An environment in which everyone is entitled and able to enjoy the good life cannot be created by market forces, but only by the body politic. The dance floor is one of the urban spaces where the body politic is constituting itself as a community transcending class, gender and colour.

I want to thank my editor at Polity, Elise Heslinga, for helping to bring about the English translation of this book eight years after it was published in German. I am indebted to my translator, Simon Pare, who enthusiastically embarked on the mission of translating this book, and found the right English words to capture the ironies and transpose the rhythms of those sometimes very long and very German sentences.

Ulrich Gutmair, May 2021

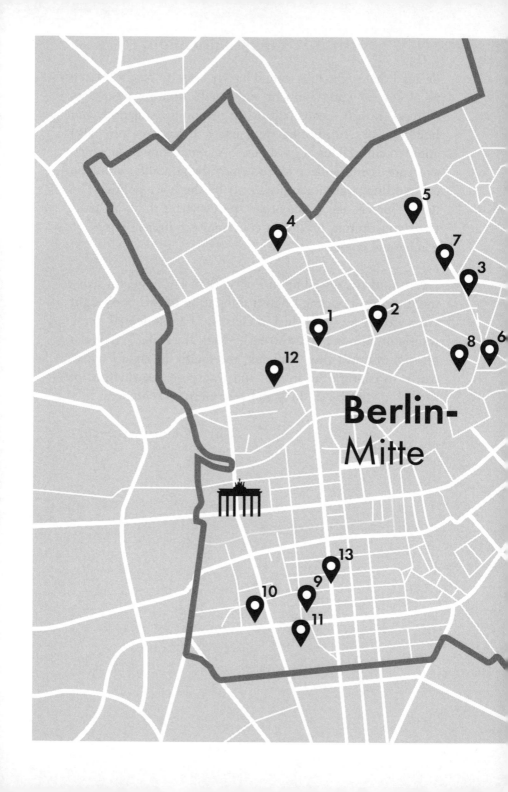

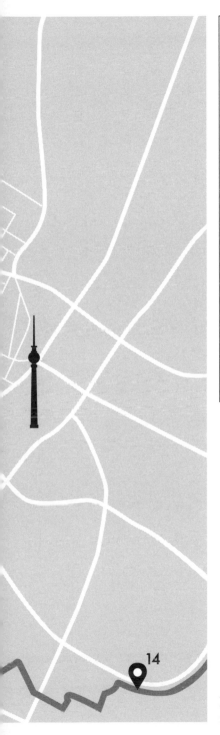

1. Tacheles, Ständige Vertretung, Obst & Gemüse
2. Galerie Wohnmaschine
3. I.M. Eimer
4. Mutzek, Panasonic
5. The Elisabethkirche
6. Gogo Bar
7. Boudoir
8. Eschloraque Rümschrümpp
9. WMF, Elektro, Sabor da Favela, Friseur
10. Tresor
11. E-Werk
12. Bunker
13. Stadtmitte underground station (U6)
14. Berlin Wall

Fig. 2 Map of Berlin showing locations mentioned in the book

1

How Long is Now?

It reeks of Bitterfeld

A Category 1 smog alert is declared if the measuring stations register too much sulphur dioxide and carbon dioxide, if those levels are sustained for three hours, and if there is a wind velocity of below 1.5 metres per second for twelve hours and an area of low pressure over the city. In such cases, residents of West Berlin are requested only to aerate their flats for a short time, not to go out walking for too long and to refrain from outdoor sport. It would probably be healthier for the inhabitants of the capital of the socialist German Democratic Republic, commonly known as East Germany, if the same guidelines were in force there. However, the thresholds are higher than in the West, which is why smog is entirely theoretical in the GDR. When a Category 1 smog alarm is declared on 1 February 1987, police patrols in West Berlin announce over 2,000 infringements of the driving ban before 11 o'clock that morning; the air in the east of the city is officially clean.

There are days when the smell of sulphur hangs in the streets, a reminder that West Berlin is surrounded by the dark continent of the Eastern Bloc, which strikes Westerners as an old, rusting, colourless industrial world populated with smoking chimneys and glum-faced proletarians operating gigantic machines. The GDR is the European country with the greatest sulphur dioxide emissions and the highest levels of particulate matter in the air. East German environmental activists complain that the chemical combine in Bitterfeld has no pollutant filter. The filters were allegedly removed from the chimneys by Soviet civil engineers after 1945 as reparations, and no new ones were ever installed. Since a pocket of air takes less than three hours on average to travel across the city, the majority of the dirt in Berlin's air is assumed not to have been caused by emissions within the city itself. As long as the power stations and factories are still operating in Czechoslovakia, Bitterfeld and Leipzig, and while people on both sides of the Wall drive cars and coal is burnt in the tiled stoves of old houses, a yellow-brown haze hangs heavily in the wintry Berlin sky whenever a south-easterly wind blows and there is a temperature inversion. The odour is unforgettable.

The deposits of these sulphurous yellow days settle on the house facades and colour them a pale shade of brown. You can see it all over town, though in West Berlin it is concentrated in poorer districts with large migrant-worker communities. In the East, where the late-nineteenth-century buildings haven't seen a lick of paint in fifty years, this brownish hue dominates the city centre. Despite being responsible for a *lack* of colour in the city, it coats your body with excess dirt. This brown suffuses your clothes after a day in the city; it turns your hands and your bathwater black. Spend the whole day outside or dance the night away in a cellar somewhere, and there'll be a black crust to scratch out of the inside of your nose the next morning. Human nostrils and building plaster are the most common magnets for the dirt in Berlin's air. At night it turns the sky orange; in homes it manifests itself as yellow ash, of which large quantities are produced from burning Rekord coal briquettes from Lusatia.

When the Wall was still there, you couldn't see it most of the time from East Berlin. A complex system of barriers, spring guns, patrols and access passes prevented the ordinary citizens of the East German capital from even approaching the 'Anti-Fascist Protective Barrier'. At night, the vacant lots and empty houses along the Wall were bathed in bright light on the eastern side. The other side of the Wall was painted in vivid colours, making it the world's largest work of street art and masking the grim East beyond.

To get a good idea of what it was like in Berlin-Mitte when it was still a little-regarded corner of the East German capital, you should take a look at Hans Martin Sewcz's photos. The photographer took some thirty black-and-white panorama photos of the streets of Mitte in May 1979. Everything is standing still; only the children are full of life, as children always are.

Two boys in shorts are advancing towards the camera. They are giving the photographer's lens a look of defiance. One of them is wearing a striped T-shirt, the other has canvas shoes on but no socks. It must have been a warm and sunny spring. Behind them lies Auguststrasse, empty and quiet. The street is clean but has obviously been repaired, creating an asphalt patchwork from different historical periods. A few Wartburgs and Trabants are parked at the side of the road. No rubbish on the pavements, no billboards on the sides of the buildings, only a laundry plying its trade. The rubble of bombed-out houses in Mitte had long since been cleared away. Small parks were established or makeshift sheds erected on those sites. The people in the photo

Fig. 3 Children in Auguststrasse, May 1979

look out of place and yet completely at home, as if they don't belong here and as if there is no life beyond these streets. Mitte is frozen in time, like the castle in Sleeping Beauty, and it stays that way until 1989, until the Politburo's sleeping spell can no longer numb the people's restiveness. When Hans Martin Sewcz photographed the streets of Mitte, East Berlin was still a romantic's paradise. Now his pictures invite the viewer to contemplate what used to be, who lived here and what the loss of that isolation means.

The Berlin winter sky is also orange one evening as we turn off Oranienburger Strasse into Tacheles' courtyard, where a Trabant is planted nose-first in the sand, a laconic memorial to a lifestyle that no longer exists. In the back wall of the house is an inconspicuous grey steel door, which opens around eleven or twelve at night. I'm not alone – nobody goes dancing on their own. Maybe there are two or three of us. We say hi to the bouncer and wink cagily at the woman on the till. She's sitting off to the right, just inside the door, huddled in a thick jacket. In front of her is a small metal box. She looks like a secretary guarding a franking machine rather than the most exciting place in Berlin. We head downstairs and step into the passageway at the bottom. The ceilings are low, the walls unplastered and damp. It smells of cellar, of decades of silence, of cigarette smoke and the spilt beer of past parties. You're confused the first time you reach this point. Which way? Straight down the tunnel into the pitch black? Or turn right, around the corner? This disorientation turns out to be a trick. There's no dark tunnel ahead of us, just a mirror standing slanted in a lift shaft. It lures you into believing in a path that doesn't exist. Then we hear the music. We turn right, around the corner, and we're inside.

An offbeat is pumping away. The bass drum pounds stoically, imperiously, at 120 beats per minute. The syncopated sound of a cymbal, running ahead, cutting in early, draws our bodies forward. Individual sounds, fat, rich and sexy, carve out spaces for themselves between the beats. Slowly our ears grow accustomed to the music. It's house, on vinyl imported from Chicago or New York. It's better, simpler and more seductive than anything we've ever heard before. People come in, stand around for a while and say hi to each other. They chat, laugh, drink beer, and then sooner or later they start dancing. They don't come here to sit around; the only seats are at the cocktail bar. Both the bar and the bar stools are mounted on springs. It's a challenge to climb up and sit down. Your legs dangle in the air as if you were swaying on the branch of a tree. It isn't very comfortable and it doesn't make sense to sit down for very long. The club consists of a damp cellar, dim light, people, music and, most importantly, motion.

You can make out two rooms, separated from one another by a smaller space in the middle. A laser beam cuts across the club from left to right, like a sign from the future encountering the remains of a story that seems to be stuck in 1945 when the Berliners hunkered down in air-raid shelters, waiting for the Red Army to arrive. A heap of rubble is a reminder of how it may once have looked down here. Further back in the dark there's a small bridge over a water-filled hole in the floor. People are dancing to a new track played by a DJ whose name we don't know. Initially, there's no DJ cult, no names you need to remember beyond the names of the places themselves. There are smells and smiles, gestures and conversations in places the music has enticed us to. There are people who move, dress, drink and smoke in their own style. They meet down here for a night in one another's company.

The club is called Ständige Vertretung. It's named after the Federal Republic of Germany's permanent diplomatic representation in East Germany which was situated just around the corner from Tacheles, in Hannoversche Strasse, from 1974, but is no longer in use. On 2 October 1990 the plaque of the 'Permanent Representation of the Federal Republic of Germany to the GDR', to give it its full name, is unscrewed and removed. From that moment on, Ständige Vertretung ceases to be a place representing a state but a place where things happen that you can only experience live. Till Vanish has hauled a few old TVs down from the street into the cellar. He uses them to show the feedback you get when you film a screen with a video camera, then play the recording on a screen and record it all over again: a permanent short circuit that produces not pictures but lighting effects. Till Vanish has a cyberpunk peroxide-blond hairstyle you can spot from a mile away. Some Sundays he cuts people's hair down here. He came from Weimar to Tacheles and lives next door.

People are dancing in the left-hand room. A French guy is at the decks, playing euphoric, minimalist music that's hard to resist. From the edge of the dance floor it looks like a private party with rules unintelligible to anyone who's only watching. Now it's all about peeling yourself away from the wall, taking that one decisive step towards the dance floor that sets everything in motion. Until your movements have become automatic and you're immersed in the music. Until you've overcome the embarrassment of letting yourself go, and the fear of looking weird. Until your mind is calm and focused, taking the occasional break, a few minutes' time out at least.

Detlef Kuhlbrodt, who used to go clubbing in Mitte, describes this moment. 'The first time I ever danced I was twelve. I'd imagined that dancing would kind of make me vanish into the here and now, but sadly that didn't really happen very often. Instead, you just felt insecure. The effort to get it right just meant the effort contaminated your movements.'

But this music, more than any other, actually makes it easier for the dancer to slip softly into it, as into sleep. House is based on loops, simple repetitive bass lines over a straightforward beat. A few sounds, a few chords played on keyboards, often imitating the sound of a piano. If there's any singing, it's generally simple commands related to dancing or to the music itself. The loops spiral forwards in time, creating a feeling, as you dance, of being fully here, an overwhelming, powerful sense of presence and simultaneity. It's the loop that moves the dancer. This produces the euphoric *je ne sais quoi* described in the 'Can you feel it?' of a famous house track, yet still unspoken, as if it were something you weren't supposed to say aloud. And so at some stage we really do vanish into the now, transported by the beats, the elegance, the lush sounds of the music, beguiled by the motions of other people's bodies, all this overspilling energy. Laughing faces, fleeting glances, attention, contact.

After we've been dancing for an hour, the sweat starts to drip on us and the others from the low ceiling where it has condensed and merged with the grimy deposits. Over the house beat, a woman's voice shouts, 'Come on!' This isn't just a memory; I can recreate it at any moment, because one of the few pieces of material evidence of my nights at Ständige Vertretung is a Scram record. It's been standing on my shelf since I bought a copy after the DJ played the Empire Mix of 'Come On' one evening. I'd taken an unforgivable peek at the turntable: sometimes sheer exuberance makes you overstep the line. That can't have been during Ständige Vertretung's first winter, though, because 'Come On' was only released on the New York-based Strictly Rhythm house label in 1992.

I have precisely three objects that are laden with memories of Ständige Vertretung. That Scram record and two slips with 'Entrance Card' printed in bold typewritten letters on thin cardboard – free entrance tickets (you saved five marks) I clearly never used. I think the cashier must have slipped them to me when I left the club in the morning, but it might have been someone else.

I moved to West Berlin in October 1989 to study at the Freie Universität. Good timing, because the Wall came down only three weeks later. In the years that followed, I spent my days at university deep in the western half of the city, while at night I was out in the unlicensed, unregistered bars, the squats and clubs of Mitte.

Memories don't work like a camera. The pictures our memory produces are hazy. They fuse with smells, sounds and faces, and in turn these are associated with conversations that might well have taken place in a completely different context. Brief moments from scattered nights over a number of years coalesce into a single memory. A riot of rapid sequences, like strobe-shattered shards that belong together but are impossible to compile into a story, however hard you may try. But I can tell when and how at least one of my first nights at Ständige Vertretung ended.

One morning, before sunrise, we staggered up the steep stairs out of the damp cellar and into the wintry orange light of Berlin. It was a Friday, 18 January 1991. The reason I'm so sure of the date is because that morning something about the big wall on the far side of the large stretch of wasteland behind Tacheles was different.

Right at the top of the wall below the roof, written in white lettering at least two metres high, was the word *KRIEG*. War. The previous evening when we went down into the Tacheles cellar – Thursday used to be house night – that graffiti hadn't been there. In the early hours of the previous day, Operation Desert Storm had begun in Iraq. That same day Helmut Kohl was elected the first chancellor of a reunified Germany.

It snowed heavily for a few days in the winter of 1990–1, making Alexanderplatz virtually impassable. The snow appeared to have got the better of East Berlin city council. The old order had collapsed, and the new one wasn't yet fully in place. A year had passed between the Wall falling and reunification. East Berlin was caught up in a turbulent transitional phase marked by constant demonstrations, art happenings and parties. A situation similar to what nineteenth-century utopians christened 'anarchy' had taken hold during the interregnum between systems; an order that appeared to function virtually without leaders. Berlin was no longer the capital of the German Empire, even though every other street corner in Mitte suggested it might have been until very recently. Berlin was no longer the capital of the GDR, and not yet the new capital of a reunified Germany. A deal for Berlin to become the capital was far from done. Quite a few people in West Germany would have much preferred the seat of government to be Bonn rather than decrepit, dirty, poor Berlin in the eastern zone, which to their minds was halfway to Siberia.

Anyone arriving for the first time in reunified Berlin from the old West Germany encountered young East Germans in the process of learning about life in a world that had changed out of all recognition. There were East Berliners coming home from Schöneberg and Kreuzberg after a brief exile. There were people who went off travelling for a long time or moved to West Germany. And then there were those who joined forces with West Berliners and new arrivals from elsewhere after the fall of the Wall to create fashion, music and art, become DJs, design flyers and set up publishing houses and galleries, organize raves, open bars and clubs, sometimes for a matter of weeks and generally with no licence to serve alcohol. The clubs were the nerve centres of the new culture of 'Metropolis Mitte', as a flyer for the Eimer, a squat in Rosenthaler Strasse, called it.

Nick Kapica and Tim Richter were keen to identify what made a good club night.

'What makes people tick? How do you get people to dance, really dance, all night long? Unlike the clubs we'd been to before, people came to us to enjoy the night. They respected the DJs as performers', Nick says. This Londoner with reddish-blond hair has Polish roots. He packed his bags when the Wall fell. The sight of all those people dancing on the Wall and the general euphoria on TV convinced him to take a look around Berlin for a year. Like so many of those who moved to Berlin-Mitte in 1990, Nick ended up in Tacheles. That was where he met the Australian Tim Richter while Café Zapata was being set up on the ground floor. One night, the two of them were hanging out, sipping their beers and wondering where they could go for a dance. They'd been to a few clubs in West Berlin, to Kreuzberg, Charlottenburg and Schöneberg, but there was something missing. A club with an idea behind it, a club that appealed to a specific audience. To their minds a club night was an event that needed curating.

Nick wanted to put into practice in Berlin what he had learned at Ravensbourne College of Design and Communication. There, they'd taught him about the Ulm School of Design's concept, based on the principles of the Bauhaus movement and the rigorous lines of Swiss modernism.

'We knew exactly what kind of public we wanted. We knew how it should feel. We knew what kind of music we'd play and we could already visualize the atmosphere inside our club', he says. 'The only thing we hadn't figured out was where to do all of this.'

Some time later, the two men knew they'd discovered the perfect place for their club when they spotted a trapdoor in the floor of Café Zapata. They shovelled out huge quantities of soot and dirt from the hole beneath it and eventually came across a flight of stairs and a walled-up door.

'It was a total mess. We structured the interior to reflect what it was like when we found it – two rooms separated by a smaller middle room. We knocked down some walls and built a bar to create a dynamic space. We didn't do any advertising in the normal sense, but every freak in Berlin came to our opening night. They became our regulars, and the line outside the door was enough to tell any future guest whether they were "in" or not', Nick Kapica says.

Initially, Ständige Vertretung only opened on Thursdays and Sundays. Those who chose to go out partying on Thursday and Sunday night, knowing full well they would have to go to work the next morning, paid for the pleasure with headaches, tiredness and below-par performance. Partying is about letting yourself go, feeling free and being unrestrained with your time. It's a good bet that most of those sipping beers and cocktails, smoking joints or snorting speed at Ständige Vertretung on a Thursday night had no regular occupation.

Nick and Tim's club was intended to be exclusive and unusual and yet open to everyone, so they chose not to apply a door policy defining who was allowed in and who wasn't. They pretended there was one, though, to create a bit of suspense.

'We were both graphic designers and that's how we approached the project', Nick says. He dreamed up slogans and themes that became the monikers of individual club nights – for example, Delirium, Swamp, Post House, Corruption and many more. You got your wrist stamped at the turnstile that marked the transition from outside rules to house rules. The day after, sometimes for a little longer, that stamp would be your only reminder of ever having been there, of having taken part in the night-time ritual. Because Ständige Vertretung operated a strict photography ban.

'Banning photos but filming people having their hair cut at night and screening it live in the club was a way of teasing out questions of secrecy and privacy. The toilets were unisex at first. No cubicles. After a while, the only feature that remained was the one-way mirror you could look out through onto the dance floor. It was all about accentuating the moment and the situation we all found ourselves in together.'

The photography ban was emphatically enforced. Breach it and your camera could end up in pieces on the floor, or at least the film torn out and exposed.

'Loads of crazy things happened in that club. The only ones who can talk about them were people who were there, and every one of them will have their own version. There are hardly any photos to back up their stories. Those people possess something special in a day and age when every event is immediately posted online. We didn't really care about being photographed, but we did want to create a special atmosphere, a sense of mystery', Nick Kapica says. 'There had to be something only people who were there could remember.'

Of the photos taken in Berlin-Mitte after the fall of the Wall most are of the streets, very few of the clubs and bars. Even when it wasn't expressly forbidden, as at Ständige Vertretung and many other clubs, it was decidedly uncool to take photos. It wasn't permitted because it is impossible to observe and take part at the same time. Walk around a club with a camera and you're like a tourist filming your own encounters. Anyone who slides a lens between themselves and the world doesn't trust their own experience. They forego the here and now in the attempt to capture a transient sensation and are immediately a nuisance to everyone else. People who abandon themselves to the DJ, the music, the beat, are revelling in the loss of control and don't appreciate being photographed in that state.

'If someone came in to take some exotic photos, we'd tell them to stop', Christoph Keller recalls. He worked the bar at the Friseur and has documented urban space in film and photographs. 'We were conscious of it being something special. We wanted to avoid any commodification of the situation. It was something we created lovingly and quite deliberately to counter that type of exploitation. It was a space for tasting freedom where there was this form of temporary protection. That was also why people put so much energy into it, without really being paid for their efforts. Friends were allowed to take photos, but we didn't like anyone doing it too openly. It would've destroyed the foundations of everything we'd built up. Some people tried to bring in video cameras, preferably with a lamp on top, but we kicked them out. It breeds alienation and ruins the atmosphere. Everyone was clear that we couldn't let it happen.'

Due to many people's aversion or simple indifference to documenting what was happening, the Berlin of those years immediately after the fall of the Wall has vanished almost without a trace. Most of the places where the old Berlin was still palpable and the new Berlin in its infancy are no longer there. There comes a point when so many tiny changes to the fabric of the city have accumulated that the essential details of the past are lost and can't be stitched back together again. The real-estate market and urban planning decisions altered the buildings, the streets and the empty plots of Mitte beyond recognition.

A lively art scene and an unbridled and all-embracing party culture emerged in Mitte in the years after the Wende – the 'turning point' around the fall of the Wall and reunification. Yet the city where this all happened now seems to have disappeared. Berlin has clothed itself in the myth of a young, tearaway city, while the substance of this profitable reputation has been gently hollowed out. Those anarchic years have become a selling point in the global competition for tourists, investors and businesses. New buildings have been erected on the vacant plots. The city centre has long since ceased to be the preserve of the squatters, ravers and artists who revived it after the fall of the Wall. The clubs have moved elsewhere, and most are now purveyors of professional entertainment. The early nineties seem like a dream you can only vaguely remember the next morning while the soundscape still echoes in your ear. The sound of the Wende encompasses not only breakbeat, house and techno but pneumatic drills and rubble chutes, the compressed scales of modems turning data into notes, nightingales singing at the best time for going out and the sound of a lark in the morning, as well as conversations on the edge of the dance floor, at gallery previews and in bars.

The man who sat by the kiosk outside Tacheles

Klaus was dead, and the kiosk was gone. Day after day he had watched over the Oranienburger Tor. He would sit there in his lumberjack shirt on his camping chair next to the kiosk, books laid out on the little table behind him, waving to people walking past and engaging them in long conversation. Now, one chill December day in 2005, there was a cardboard sign leaning against the side of the kiosk with his photo and the words *Klaus is dead* on it. Someone had placed candles and flowers in front of the sign. Alongside them were offerings of bottles of beer and vodka to accompany him on his journey into the realm of the dead.

A little while after Klaus Fahnert died, the kiosk vanished too – it's visible next to the advertising column on 1950s black-and-white photos – and also the nearby snack stand. The small triangular space on the corner of Linienstrasse and Oranienburger Strasse where Klaus spent his days has been recobbled. It has looked clean and tidy ever since, as if this were a typical West German town grown fat on prosperous decades. Klaus lived in Mitte for fifteen years, for nearly ten of which he was to be found sitting next to Serdar Yildirim's kiosk, diagonally across the road from Tacheles.

Serdar Yildirim is a small, wiry man with dark shoulder-length hair. It took me a while to track down the former leaseholder of the old kiosk at Oranienburger Tor, though he wasn't far away. After much enquiring, the friendliest vendor at Dada Falafel told me that the people from the kiosk had moved to the other side of the street. Serdar has set up shop in a repurposed shipping container next to Tacheles and sells articles such as postcards and T-shirts to tourists. He generally works nights. Serdar had known Klaus since late 1996.

'Klaus was fit as a flea back then', he says. 'He walked up, stopped in front of the kiosk and asked for a beer. He told me he was married, had children and loved this part of town. That's how we met. Then he started coming every day and one day he asked if he could sit next to the kiosk and sell a few books. I said, I don't mind. If it doesn't bother the wardens, it doesn't bother me. He originally came from Bonn and whenever he saw the letters BN on a numberplate, he'd say, "That stands for Berlin Next." Daytimes aren't very busy in summer, not many customers, so I'd often sit down with him for a chat', Serdar says, lighting another cigarette.

By the time Klaus claimed his patch at Oranienburger Tor, Berliners and tourists in the know had long since moved on to other parts of the city to party. Tacheles was just a pesky hangover. The walls of the staircase were sprayed with coat after coat of graffiti, one on top of the other, tags stretching back to the palaeolithic era of the Berlin Republic, the first days and weeks after the fall of the Wall. It stank of beer and urine. Hawkers sold handicrafts on the first floor, and young Italians, Spaniards and Swedes sat in Café Zapata, trying to feel how Berlin must once have felt. For people from the neighbourhood, Klaus was part of the local furniture, whereas for most of the passers-by on their way to the underground station he was presumably just another dosser, lounging around in his camping chair in broad daylight next to a table of books. Klaus was a good fit with Tacheles, which had become one of new Berlin's international tourist landmarks along with the Television Tower.

Approaching from the east, the party wall of Tacheles is visible from a long way off. It is painted with a large, vague likeness of a woman's face, and above it is a question: 'How long is now?' Is the present a mathematically non-expansible point in the stream of time that divides the past from the future, or is it more than that? The tourists you see ambling along Oranienburger Strasse have time for now. They wander around taking photos, clearly fascinated by Kunsthaus Tacheles. It's a bit messy but colourful, slightly dilapidated yet alive. Which is what people all over the world imagine Berlin to be like.

How long is now? It's a question that sums up handily the spirit of the Wende, the tumultuous years before and after the East German revolution, the sense of a new departure laden with immense possibilities. Now is always. Life is in the present. Tourists intuitively grasp that. However, when they stand gazing at Tacheles and the large piece of empty land around the building, they see more than that. An old wound is being kept open here. Entering East Berlin from the West in 1989, you felt yourself catapulted back into the immediate post-war years; you were moving through an open-air museum. Nothing had been buried, everything lay uncovered. You could engage in archaeology simply by walking around.

Then and for many years afterwards, the wastelands and the scarred house fronts showed that soldiers fought, right here, in the middle of the city. The walls were still pitted with bullet holes from the Battle of Berlin in April 1945. Visitors to Tacheles didn't need to know that the former shopping arcade and department store were used by the Deutsche Arbeitsfront (the Nazi-endorsed German Labour Front, which replaced independent trade unions) and by the SS, or that French prisoners of war toiled away up in the attics. Directly after the fall of the Wall, there was no need for tour guides or information panels to convey the history of Berlin-Mitte. The history of the twentieth century was written into the cityscape – all you had to do was look. 'Now' means all the experiences, memories and history present at a given moment in time.

Around noon on 13 February 1990 Leo Kondeyne, Clemens Wallrodt and their friends pull up in an old fire engine outside what remains of the former department store in the Oranienburger Strasse. The squatters climb onto the roof of their vehicle and in through a first-floor window. It is evident from the back of the building that the GDR's demolition experts carried out their task with great precision. They blew up the majority of the sprawling complex around its central dome because the East German capital's urban planners wanted to build a street here. The building was still in use in the 1970s. The squatters stand in the large empty space behind the building and stare up into open rooms that have been cut in half.

The complex was built by Franz Ahrens between 1907 and 1909 using reinforced concrete in the modern style. A glass-roofed shopping arcade connected the large and still extant entrance arch on Oranienburger Strasse with Friedrichstrasse, and at its central point the arcade opened up into a dome. However, the idea of competing with the major department stores by linking a cluster of specialized shops to a centralized till system, thus making shopping easier, failed after only a year; the arcade-cum-department store closed down in 1914. In 1928 the building was acquired by the electrical company AEG, which renamed it Haus der Technik and exhibited its latest products in the spacious and luxurious showrooms. The first vacuum cleaners in Berlin were supposedly sold here.

In 1933 Nazi organizations began to occupy parts of the building. It was later damaged during Allied bombing raids on the capital of the Third Reich. The bomb damage report for 16 December 1943, filed by Berlin's anti-air-raid headquarters, indicates that the Haus der Technik was hit during the 160th bombing raid. Two hundred and fifty planes had flown over the city at around 7:30 that evening. The building sustained further bomb damage in 1944.

After the founding of the German Democratic Republic, it was used by the Free German Trade Union Federation and the College of Foreign Trade. The Oranienburger Tor Lichtspiele, a picture house, opened in the building first, followed by the Studio Camera Berlin, the cinema of the state film archive. A branch of the Berlin savings bank and a lingerie shop also moved in. The large cellars were later flooded for structural reasons, and in the early 1980s demolition work commenced.

The squatters occupy the building prior to the first free East German parliamentary elections in March, its scheduled demolition in April and the East Berlin city council assembly elections in May 1990. Construction workers place dynamite into the blast holes by day, and at night the squatters fish it out again. The squatters name the building Tacheles after the free jazz combo of which some of them are members. They are based at Rosenthaler Strasse 68, known as the Eimer because the squatters apparently found buckets in every room. Its full name is I.M. Eimer, meaning literally 'in the bucket' or, more idiomatically, 'shafted'. But I.M. also stands for 'inoffizieller Mitarbeiter' ('informal collaborator') – someone who was either forced to act as an informant for the Stasi, the East German secret service, or did so out of conviction.

The stand-alone building (there are empty plots on either side) was occupied on 17 January 1990, almost a month before Tacheles, by members of the East German bands Freygang, Ich-Funktion and Die Firma, and their mates. A flyer addressed to the 'dear people' of Mitte reads: 'Since no one seems bothered by the disintegration of many buildings, we, a collective of three rock bands, have taken full responsibility for the house at Rosenthaler Strasse 68.' They said they were appropriating the building out of 'euphoria for the present moment'. They would insulate the building for sound and respect the interests of local residents. The squatters proclaimed the house an autonomous cultural centre and established an association called Operative Behavioural Art. Its logo is a giant ear mounted on the roof.

One of the starting points for the occupation of the Eimer was the house at Schönhauser Allee 5. It was home to Autonome Aktion Wydoks, one of whose leaders was Aljoscha Rompe. The stepson of Robert Rompe, the communist resistance fighter, plasma physicist and member of the central committee of the SED (the Socialist Unity Party that ruled East Germany throughout its existence), Aljoscha Rompe founded the GDR's first official punk band. Feeling B toured the country for years. Concerts in the province were followed by parties, some lasting for days. Feeling B responded to people's constant griping about scarcities in East Germany with out-and-out hedonism. It wasn't their political lyrics that irked the authorities but their refusal to toe the line regarding socialism's world-historical mission; they preferred to party and mess about. The lyrics of one of their tracks, 'Graf Zahl' ('The Count of Numbers'), are a long list of numbers, starting at one and stopping only when the band feels the song has gone on long enough. Two of the members of Feeling B soon moved on to found Rammstein, who once performed at the Eimer before becoming an international synonym for gloomy German pop.

Aljoscha Rompe died in 2000 from an asthma attack in his camper van. An obituary had the following to say about Rompe's role in the years after the fall of the Wall: 'He held court at Schönhauser Allee 5 in Prenzlauer Berg, a house that was squatted before the Wende then quickly legalized through tenancy agreements, and came to illustrate in microcosm the Prenzlauer Berg scene's attempt to conquer the West and its failure to do so. Thanks to Aljoscha, the Schönhauser Allee house became a hub for East Berlin left-wingers, with concerts in the courtyard, its own pirate radio station up in the attic, a cinema in the cellar and lots of drinking in makeshift bars with a shabby living-room charm. These good-time *guerilleros* had the cheek to tap into public funds and build a recording studio, and Autonome Aktion Wydoks fell only a few votes short of winning seats on the district council.'

Autonome Aktion Wydoks received 824 votes in the East Berlin local elections. The monthly membership fee was five marks, and the statutes said that anyone 'not too flabby or floppy and able to withstand a constant barrage of at least 150 phons of music at our bar' could join, according to the German news magazine *Der Spiegel*. Immediately after the Wende, while it was still a loose association of East German punks and not yet a party, the Aktion called for people to grab empty houses in East Berlin first before others got there.

The flyer announcing the occupation of the Eimer in Rosenthaler Strasse concluded with the words 'From Wednesday, Berlin will be a cultural metropolis. People of the world, hear the signal!' It was meant as a joke, but it was still accurate. The squatters chose buildings in strategic spots. One of the heartlands of this future cultural metropolis was in the old Spandauer Vorstadt, a former suburb between Tacheles and the Eimer diagonally bisected by two parallel streets – the neighbourhood's main thoroughfare, Auguststrasse, and Linienstrasse. The Scheunenviertel (Barn Quarter), part of the Spandauer Vorstadt, and the Rosenthaler Vorstadt north of Torstrasse were also part of the new district of Mitte. Many artists were attracted to live and work there because there was ample room for ateliers and temporary art projects that either cost nothing, being squats, or were cheap by virtue of being available on temporary licence.

The streets of Spandauer Vorstadt had always been home to upstanding citizens alongside nightclubs and brothels. Leo Heller wrote of Linienstrasse in 1928 that it was 'the main artery of a neighbourhood traditionally associated with crooks'. But it wouldn't be right to call these roads mean streets, he noted, because 'strangely, the nastiest and most notorious areas of Berlin are also home to an honest, solidly middle-class population'. Heller mentioned Linienstrasse being the territory of 'adventurous ladies and their protectors'. The road was lined with hotels, student bars and dives such as Zur Melone, frequented exclusively by burglars. In the late nineteenth century, the Eimer building in Rosenthaler Strasse housed a popular bar called Der Blaue Panther with an adjacent brothel. Prostitution returned to Oranienburger Strasse the summer before the fall of the Wall: the whores were a few months ahead of the revolution. The galleries, bars and clubs that appeared in the neighbourhood soon afterwards foreshadowed its future as a desirable and expensive part of the city.

Fig. 4 Wrecked car in Auguststrasse, 1990

Mitte's importance as a location for galleries dated back to the days of East Germany. Friedrich Loock started his first gallery in early 1989 in his small flat in Tucholskystrasse before later moving Wohnmaschine to shop premises in the same building. Legend has it that it was he who came up with the idea in the winter of 1989 of organizing an exhibition in the old shopping arcade in Oranienburger Strasse that was squatted and named Tacheles soon afterwards. When the Wall came down, Kunst-Werke opened its doors in Auguststrasse. Judy Lybke's gallery Eigen + Art took up residence a few buildings away, allgirls gallery was diagonally opposite and for a while Galerie Neu ran a few rooms at the other end of the street. A sculptor opened Hackbarths in Auguststrasse, a corner pub that is still there today. And so, after the fall of the Wall, a web of galleries, bars and clubs quickly came into existence. Art was also the ongoing result of productive hang-outs in bars run and frequented by artists, places where they could share ideas with colleagues, critics and gallery owners.

There was certainly no shortage of opportunities for such conversations at the counters of bars and on the edge of the dance floors in Mitte. Dozens of bars and small clubs sprang up in the area bounded by Chausseestrasse in the west and Alexanderplatz in the east, Oranienburger Strasse and Invalidenstrasse in the south and north. Clustered around Hackescher Markt were Aktionsgalerie, Assel, C-base, Eschloraque Rümschrümpp, the berlin-tokyo gallery, the Gogo Bar, Sniper and Toaster, and in Rosenthaler Strasse you could find Club for Chunk, Delicious Doughnuts and the Eimer; there was Sexiland and the Imbiss International snack stand on Rosenthaler Platz, and the Boudoir, the Glowing Pickle, Hohe Tatra and Subversiv in Brunnenstrasse; Ackerstrasse had Schokoladen, and then there was Acud in Veteranenstrasse, and Suicide Circus in

Dircksenstrasse. Mutzek in Invalidenstrasse subsequently became the Panasonic. There was a whole array of Monday bars. For a while 103 took up residence near Oranienburger Strasse, as did the fourth and fifth iterations of WMF, which had been hopping around the city since 1990. People went to Kunst + Technik on the banks of the river Spree opposite the Museumsinsel.

This is only a selection of local clubs. Some stuck around for long enough to become fixtures, some existed for a single summer or winter and others for just one party; very few have survived to this day. Some places quickly made the listings in the city's magazines, others you could only find if you knew the right people or happened to be in the right place at the right time. Flyers publicized parties and exhibition previews. Sometimes music and loud voices would lure you into a courtyard as you were walking past, and you would stand there outside a house, in a courtyard, by a door, listening out for where the party was. The best plan for someone unfamiliar with the neighbourhood was to get out of the underground at Oranienburger Tor and start their tour at Café Zapata or Obst & Gemüse.

Serdar's cousin was the first Yildirim here. He opened his snack stand in April 1993. The small building used to be a public toilet in East Germany, perhaps even in Hitler's day. Now Serdar's cousin supplied the locals and the Tacheles squatters on the other side of the road with doner kebabs, boreks, multivitamin juice and beer until four or five in the morning.

Serdar's family soon took over the kiosk next door. Magazines and newspapers were spread on the wide shelves in front of the glass-fronted stall, and tobacco and drinks passed out through the large window. Serdar was fourteen when he started to lend his parents a hand. When he first took his place at the news stand, Café Zapata had opened at Tacheles diagonally opposite, Obst & Gemüse a little further on. People used to drop peanut shells on the floor there, and by the early hours a layer an inch deep would have formed. They drank beer from the bottle standing up, as had long become the custom in Kreuzberg and Schöneberg. In the summer, squatters from Mitte would sit at the tables and on the pavement alongside guests from all over the world. Obst & Gemüse and Café Zapata were there before any other pubs had really got going in Mitte.

'The Zapata and Obst & Gemüse were enough at the time. The street was busier then than it is now', Serdar says. 'People lived in Tacheles and in the building next door. The whole thing was all open, and anyone could just go in and out. There were hundreds of people, from England, Ireland, Spain, Italy, West Germany and East.'

Many others were also involved in German reunification. Serdar's list could be a lot longer. Totting up the nationalities, he left out the young Americans, Austrians, Australians, Yugoslavs, Poles, Russians, Lithuanians, Finns, Dutch and other overwhelmingly young visitors for whom Tacheles was a gateway into a different land after the fall of the Wall. This was a place where sometime sightseers became squatters, passers-by became partakers, rovers evolved into ravers and middle-class kids got creative. Tacheles was the interface between the official city and the uncharted territory of Berlin-Mitte with its squats, temporary studios and bars, improvised living-room galleries and nomadic basement clubs.

The reunification of West Berlin and the former East German capital was sealed on the dance floor and in bars, at previews and in beds in occupied houses. Everyone in Mitte came from somewhere, which was equally true of the people who'd gone nowhere. The citizens of the capital of the GDR stayed in the same place. They shut the door behind them one evening, went to sleep and woke up the next morning in a different city. The people who drove out the Politburo in the autumn of 1989 and occupied the Stasi's Normannenstrasse headquarters during the winter were desperate to see the world beyond the Wall, but within months the whole world had come to them. The streets of Mitte echoed to the sound of English, Spanish, Italian and Russian. Given that a majority of East Germans couldn't speak any English, most of the foreign pioneers quickly picked up a smattering of German to be able to chat, shop and order food at a snack bar.

In his 1992 documentary film *Aufgestanden in Ruinen* [*Risen in Ruins*], Klaus Tuschen presents the early days of Art House Tacheles. He shows how an open commune develops into a cultural venue, how a social structure morphs into a subsidized institution. We watch people arguing in plenary sessions and the house's spokesman taking government minister Rita Süssmuth on a guided tour, describing the various cultural activities in his audibly Swabian accent and informing her about the ongoing repairs. The minister is in a good mood and obviously enthused. Less impressed by the in-house developments are a group of East German punks, including a child, who feel bullied. The professionalization and institutionalization of the house are good for the artists and theatre professionals who plan to work here. The punks, who just want to live and party in the building, are already in the way. In the middle of this laboratory – a microcosm of the way Mitte is heading – a construction squad of young Brits, Australians and Americans is on the job. They sit in front of the camera in their sturdy boots and dusty clothes and explain how they want to remove all the rubble from Tacheles' cellar so that it can host one of the first clubs in Mitte: Ständige Vertretung.

'We couldn't do this in London or any of the other cities we come from. That's why this is happening in Berlin', a reddish-haired Brit says.

His American mate says, 'None of what we're doing here is forever. Whatever you do in life, it's only ever temporary.' But Tacheles is more than a squat. 'It's a monument to the East German squatter movement.'

The Tacheles squatters bought cigarettes from Serdar Yildirim, and he made friends with some of them. From time to time, he would have a beer at Café Zapata after work.

'Once, when I was taking a taxi home at four in the morning, I saw Klaus outside the shop. He'd set up his stall and was just sitting there. The weather made no difference to him. I had an awning and so if it rained, he'd move his stand over to the side of the shop where he wouldn't get wet.'

Serdar says that Klaus Fahnert used to sleep in an empty plot just around the corner in Torstrasse.

'That's where he used to store his books. He would comb skips for books and old lamps. He didn't really sell them. He gave a lot of things away. Many people donated a few marks or bought him a beer. Begging wasn't his style. He was very popular in the street, and all the kids knew him. He often ate at the snack stand, and lots of people, not just people from the bakery or the pizzeria on the corner, used to give him food. Almost every day, the nice waitress from the German pub opposite would bring him something to eat, with sauerkraut and potatoes, all wrapped up. Klaus talked to people, and lots of people liked talking to him. He was no idiot. He was pretty smart actually. He'd talk politics. His nickname was "Mr Mayor". Joschka Fischer often came here to buy something in his funny hat.'

Joschka Fischer, the former agitator of a fairly unsuccessful attempt to organize workers at the Opel car factory in

Rüsselsheim, a militant member of the Revolutionärer Kampf group in Frankfurt, taxi driver, translator and actor, was vice chancellor and foreign minister of the Federal Republic of Germany when he stopped off for something at Serdar's kiosk in the early 2000s. He lived in Tucholskystrasse. His building was three minutes by foot heading down Oranienburger Strasse from the kiosk towards the synagogue.

'He knew Klaus and would always chat to him for quite a while. That's why I like Joschka Fischer – he didn't look down his nose at people', Serdar says. 'He always had a look at the books Klaus had and would often buy something. Whether he read them is another matter.'

Klaus Fahnert liked wearing badges on his lumberjack shirts. A TV reporter was struck by one saying 'Stop Stoiber' two days before the federal elections in September 2002 when Edmund Stoiber, the head of the Bavarian Christian Social Union party, was trying to dislodge the incumbent red–green government led by Gerhard Schröder and Joschka Fischer. Since Klaus was supposed to represent the homeless people of Mitte in her report and was displaying political messages, the journalist asked if he voted. To which Klaus's answer was: 'Your princes are rogues and layabouts. I would abhor voting for you.' These are the only words ever spoken by Klaus Fahnert that show up on the internet.

There's a photo of Klaus hanging right next to the door of Serdar's new kiosk.

'Klaus was actually quite happy with his life', Serdar says. 'But you know how it ended?'

The vacant plots vanish

A homeless man dying, a kiosk vanishing from urban landscape: these are events of no interest to historians. Cities are sites of constant change. People die all the time. Other people get out of cars, trains and planes and seek their place in the city. Some spend a weekend partying in Berlin's clubs. Some buy a flat and go home again – back to Stuttgart, to the prosperous shores of Lake Starnberg, to Milan, Barcelona or Stockholm. Some stay for a while, others stay for good. When larger communities arrive, such as the Huguenots, the Jews or the Turks, they change the face of the city. The fact that guys like Klaus are part of city life too is an insufficient reason to study them, apparently. It is symptomatic, however, that there used to be space for someone like Klaus in the middle of a city, and yet that space no longer seems to exist.

For many first-hand witnesses to the breakneck pace of change after the fall of the Wall, the transformation formed a significant part of their life stories, but they also found it an odd experience. It's uncanny living in a city you could tell many stories about if only you could mould them into a narrative.

That was Brad's experience (full name Sung-Uk Bradden Hwang). In 1990 this art student, who grew up in rural Utah, moved from Los Angeles to Berlin, where he didn't know a soul. He had no money and he didn't speak German. Brad used junk to build gadgets whose function was determined by the meaning observers ascribed to them. He viewed his artworks as gifts: 'Giving away the very things you don't have to people who can't pay for them.'

Brad constructed a potato-waffle-throwing machine from a trolley normally used for transporting bottles of welding gas. He made a portable lightning machine. For Café Zapata at Tacheles he built 'The Singing, Soup-Cooking Heating System' out of steel barrels, its secondary function being to heat the café. A reporter from *Der Spiegel* noted in 1991 that the artwork created something of a stir. When the journalist asks him why he came to Berlin, Brad doesn't understand the question. 'Hier isset, man' ('This is where it's at, man') is his comment – he'd picked up Berlin dialect and specific countercultural slang in record time. The new energy, unification – 'It's one helluva fix', he says.

Twenty years on, Brad is still in Berlin. He, his wife and their two kids live on a houseboat called *Odin*. In 2011 he posted a text titled 'Ghost Investigation' online. In it he tries to explain why there is so little record of his work from the period after the Wall fell. His conclusion is that it wasn't necessary.

'When all's said and done, we would collect food and junk in the mornings, visit friends before lunch (and scribble something on the door if they weren't in) to talk about that day and the weather and everything else in life, make music for a bit around noon, hook up to the neighbours' running hot water in the afternoons, cook a meal and eat together in the evenings, dance the nights away, sleep. The next day we would go looking for coal briquettes, queue up outside with a phone we'd found or borrowed to connect it to a recently discovered working line, organize or play at or go to a gig, paint or look at pictures, sleep for a bit longer the day after that, make music again or DJ, more cooking and eating, no hot water after all, try again.' How are you meant to document all those things when artistic production is such an integral part of an unfathomable routine, Brad wonders. 'No matter, tomorrow's another day.'

He's still haunted by the ghosts of the post-Wende years. 'Where have Mayakovsky's wonderful life or Beuys's social sculptures gone? Where has the classless society gone? Didn't something happen? We sensed the ghosts in the darkness, on the edges of our vision, again and again, in moments of upheaval and unrest, but we cannot grasp them. The normal strategy seems to be to explain them away. Atemporality should at last be recorded as history; at the end of the day, it's the only thing we can embrace, archive, sell or forget.' Brad Hwang quotes Octavio Paz: 'Anyone who has looked hope in the eye will never be able to forget it. He will search for it wherever he goes.' Brad Hwang thinks these ghosts wouldn't haunt us if they didn't have something important to whisper to us.

Klaus is one such ghost. You would often see him standing by the bar in Elektro at Mauerstrasse 15, three underground stations from Oranienburger Tor, before he started sitting by the kiosk opposite Tacheles. The vacant plots next to the Elektro were covered with grasses and fast-spreading invasive plants, the prettiest and most conspicuous of which was staghorn sumac. The staghorn, known to botanists as *Rhus hirta* or *Rhus typhina*, belongs to the *Anacardiaceae* family. It was introduced to Europe from North America in 1602 and first planted in Germany in 1676. It has now spread across the entire country. It has light-coloured wood and is easy to recognize from afar by its feathery leaves. It thrives in Berlin's sandy soil, its roots forming rambling rhizomes.

There was constant building going on in Berlin. Wherever, not so long ago, there had been a vacant site, full of grasses and staghorn sumac, wherever no gardener was keeping things in check because the site's ownership was unclear, wherever heirs were at loggerheads, speculation was rife or an investor had gone bankrupt years ago: a couple of weeks later, the foundations of a new building would have been poured. The empty plots disappeared under the new buildings, taking the staghorn and the memories with them.

The disappearance of the gaps and holes in Mitte refutes many historians' claims that only remembering is a productive process and that forgetting befalls us automatically. The vacant plots reminded Mitte's residents of the destruction of the war. Their loss represented the loss of a historic space, an amnesia that corroded the urban environment. While he was alive, Klaus was both a witness and living testament to the fact that all of this had once existed on the corner of Mauerstrasse and Kronenstrasse, where an office block now stands and nothing remains to remind people that this was once one of the liveliest, most productive places in Mitte.

'I find it hard to remember the places I used to go and what they looked like', Christoph Keller says. 'I've really blocked it all out. I'd love to climb inside one of those ghost houses now and take a look around. I also get the years muddled up. Later, they put up scaffolding in front of the houses, and it would be in place for a year. Then they'd take it down again and behind it there'd be something completely new. It's like after a war: I can't reconnect with the old geography.'

People have different opinions about what happened to the city after the Wall came down. Regarding what came next, though, there is one thing all Mitte's residents can quickly agree upon: it is impossible to square the memories with the reality.

'This happens repeatedly throughout history', Christoph Keller says. 'People repress memories after wars or other periods of upheaval. A similar thing has happened here because there's been such a turnover in the population of Mitte and because the buildings are no longer here to bear witness. It all happened so fast. By the end of the nineties, you could only talk in the past tense.'

The disappearance of the vacant plots was symptomatic of this repression in two ways: where the vacant sites were redeveloped, forgetting began; and where the gaps were still visible or people remembered them, conversations began.

2

The Year of Anarchy

The Mitte Temporary Autonomous Zone

Raquel Eulate crossed the border illegally. She squeezed through a hole in the Wall on Bernauer Strasse, three minutes from Voltastrasse underground station in Wedding district.

'A few months after the fall of the Wall, foreigners still weren't allowed to stay overnight in East Berlin', she says. 'Some people I knew were living in a house in Dunckerstrasse. Tacheles, the Eimer and various other squats already existed. I would sometimes stay in the East for a few days and then slip back through a hole in the Wall into West Berlin. This Londoner had told me about it. He'd been roaming around East Berlin when he heard about a hole in the Wall where you could come and go as you liked. When I told my friends in West Berlin, they said, "You're nuts, Raquel. The border's a minefield." I said there were lots of rabbits there and it was all right. I always went on my own. I wasn't scared.

When you went over to Mitte, everyone was nice to you. I always felt welcome.'

Most East Berliners had few opportunities to meet people from the West. Another advantage Raquel had was that she was a young white woman. The only thing that might have raised the suspicions of the young Nazis prowling around Mitte were her dreadlocks – the eighties had only just come to an end and a new fashion was yet to catch on.

Raquel is originally from Spain and never really learned German properly because she was only in Mitte for four years – she moved from Berlin to London in 1994. As a foreigner who couldn't speak the language, she stood little chance of being able to study in Germany in the 1990s. So she found a college in London where she could take a course, then began working with computers and now earns her living as a web designer. In the summer of 2012, she moved back to Berlin.

She rattles off her story as fast in English as she would in her mother tongue.

Raquel planned to squat a house with some friends. 'I definitely wanted to go to East Berlin. As a foreigner in West Berlin, I had no particular attachment to the place. It was much more interesting in the East. You could pick out the best buildings, and it was rent-free. You could live in nice places, start a commune and do art projects instead of sitting all by yourself in a West Berlin flat.'

People who went over to the other side from West Berlin in 1990 entered a world of new opportunities. To cross the border was to experience how social pressures lost the power you'd always regarded as innate in them; they meant nothing here. Why live alone if you could live together? Why pay rent when you could live free of charge in a squat? Why go to work when you could make art? Why watch films and read novels when, every day and every night, you could talk to people, listen to music, party and have new experiences?

Fig. 5 Living room at Kleine Hamburger Strasse 5 in early 1991

Some of the new inhabitants in 1990 disappeared into Mitte like the white men and women sent out as settlers from England to the New World. Instead of working hard every day, surveying, mapping and appropriating the new country, suffering hunger and starvation, they ran off into the forest and joined the 'savages'.

That is Hakim Bey's version of the history of North America's first 'Lost Colony' in in his book *T.A.Z.: The Temporary Autonomous Zone: Ontological Anarchy, Poetic Terrorism.*[1] On its publication in 1991, Berliners read it as a description of what was taking place in their own city.

Every American schoolchild knows the mythical tale of the 'Lost Colony'. At the end of the sixteenth century, Elizabeth I granted Sir Walter Raleigh a charter to establish a colony in North America. The first British settlement was founded

---

[1] Hakim Bey is the occasional pen name of Peter Lamborn Wilson (b. 1945), an American anarchist author and poet.

on the island of Roanoke off the coast of present-day North
Carolina. The colonists were soldiers and investigators.
They came ashore at a time of great drought, bringing with
them diseases that swelled into epidemics. They torched
entire villages for trifling reasons. Their mission was a failure, and most of the colonists sailed back to England. New
settlers arrived, but this time there were families among
them. Virginia Dare was the first British child born on
North American soil, the granddaughter of John White, the
colony's governor, who sought to come to a peaceful arrangement with the local tribes. When the colony once more fell
into severe hardship, White left the island to fetch help from
England. Almost three years later, on 18 August 1590, his
granddaughter's birthday, he arrived back in Roanoke to find
the colony abandoned. The colonists had vanished after first
dismantling their houses – a sign that they were not forced
to flee. The only thing John White found was a message:
someone had carved the word 'Croatoan' on a stake in the
fort's palisade.

Presenting his text on the 'Temporary Autonomous
Zone' at the Jack Kerouac School of Disembodied Poetics
in Boulder, Colorado, four hundred years later, Hakim Bey
offered his own particular interpretation of the story of the
Lost Colony:

We were taught in elementary school that the first settle-
ments in Roanoke failed; the colonists disappeared, leaving
behind them only the cryptic message 'Gone To Croatan'.
Later reports of 'grey-eyed Indians' were dismissed as
legend. What really happened, the textbook implied, was
that the Indians massacred the defenseless settlers. However,
'Croatan' was not some Eldorado; it was the name of a
neighboring tribe of friendly Indians. Apparently, the settlement was simply moved back from the coast into the Great

Dismal Swamp and absorbed into the tribe. And the grey-eyed Indians were real – they're *still there*, and they still call themselves Croatans.

The colonists had cancelled their agreement with the British Empire. 'They dropped out. They became "Indians", "went native".'

Hakim Bey believes that Americans had had this same yearning for the wild, a return to the state of nature, ever since. The possibility of leaving farm work, church, education and taxes behind them has lingered on in the American consciousness, and the dream of becoming an Indian is an indelible feature of American culture to this day.

With his concept of Temporary Autonomous Zones, the US anarchist was trying to answer the question of how to enjoy the fruits of a revolution that never happens. 'Are we who live in the present doomed never to experience autonomy, never to stand for one moment on a bit of land ruled only by freedom? Are we reduced either to nostalgia for the past or nostalgia for the future?', as Bey wrote in *T.A.Z.* Bey believed that there is a third option. His answer is the 'poetic fantasy' of a 'guerrilla operation that liberates a piece of land, time or imagination and then dissolves to reappear elsewhere'. He called this fantasy a 'Temporary Autonomous Zone' or 'TAZ'. Bey detected forerunners of the TAZ in the Caribbean pirate republics, the Bavarian Soviet Republic of 1918–19 and the Spanish anarchist experiment, which was contested from the left and the right and brought to a brutal end by the civil war that broke out in 1936. Bey even saw the short-lived Free State of Fiume after the First World War as an example of a TAZ, paying scant attention to the fascist tendencies of this republic and its leader, the Italian poet Gabriele D'Annunzio. Bey was more interested in the fact that D'Annunzio wrote a constitution for his city of Fiume that declared music to be the organizing principle of the state.

T.A.Z.: The Temporary Autonomous Zone fell on fertile ground in Berlin. The book circulated among anarchists, computer nerds, cyberpunks, squatters, intellectuals, artists and ravers. Its appeal to many readers was that it offered a ready-made pick-and-mix of enticing arguments for the possibility of short instants of authentic living amid all the fakery. The promised intensification of everyday life made sense to a generation that had grown up with pop culture. For readers interested in computer networks it offered an analysis of the internet's potential. The anarchism Bey proposed is practical and mystical: humans should be intoxicated and joyful. Ravers in Mitte required no second invitation. However, it was Bey's idea of occupying gaps in space and time that appeared to be the most persuasive summary of the situation in East Berlin after the fall of the Wall, and so the idea of Temporary Autonomous Zones became a watchword. It epitomized the romantic and naïve – yet in the circumstances hardly far-fetched – idea that here, for a while, people could do, or not do, whatever they chose.

Bey defined the twentieth century as the period when there were no more blank spots left on the map. The last little bit of unclaimed land had been seized by a nation-state in 1899; and then, at the very moment Bey was telling his readers this, the Eastern Bloc collapsed. This supported the hypothesis that even after the last piece of terra incognita had been mapped, the possibility of exerting total control over every expanse of land was entirely theoretical: the map is not the territory, and gathering every scrap of data about an area is not the same as governing it. The old map of East Berlin was obsolete. The fall of the Wall spelled the end of a social system. Real existing socialism was bankrupt. There was a territory in the East just waiting to be remodelled, its uncertain temporary state simply to be experienced or enjoyed for as long as it remained unclear who owned what. Until the investors had made their play. By the summer of 1990, just over 130 buildings in East Berlin had been converted into squats.

The first time Raquel Eulate sneaked through the hole in the Wall, she quickly worked out where the squats were. There weren't many in East Berlin in the winter months after the fall of the Wall; you could locate them simply by wandering around a bit. She waited for an opportunity to claim a place.

'Someone at Tacheles tipped us off that there was a nice flat in a house in Invalidenstrasse. He led me, Yvonne Harder and a third person there. We got in via the courtyard. Once inside, though, we realized it stretched all the way through to Invalidenstrasse. It was a big, beautiful building. I lived there at the start with Yvonne Harder, who ran her space, Mutzek, on the ground floor.'

Mutzek's premises comprised 'three partially tiled exhibition rooms, a common room or lounge, a bar and a coatroom that was used as a butcher's up until two years ago', according to Mutzek's own profile in a publication by the Berlin-Mitte housing association and the Mitte cultural office in 1993. This guide is as fat as a phone book and printed on cheap paper that had already yellowed twenty years later. It is a compendium of all the cultural institutions and projects in Mitte.

Mutzek's proprietors are listed as Martha and Maria Mutzek, who present themselves as *salonnières*: 'The salons of the last century were places where writers, artists, musicians and philosophers could regularly meet and converse in the homes of society ladies with the space, the time and the possibility – due to their social status – to host this kind of get-together.' The fictional Mutzek sisters had enough space and time and no need for 'social status'. They did, however, reside in a former bourgeois house. Some of the first-floor rooms were separated by large sliding doors, and a few apartments had their own servants' quarters. A small staircase led to an intermediate storey – the ceilings there were just high enough to stand upright – where the maids lived.

The luxury of the pre-war era was now available to all. Everyone in Mitte was at liberty to devote themselves to the good things in life, including conversation; anyone could host a salon.

Yvonne Harder was familiar with this counterculture where bohemians from the East met newcomers from the West. 'In the intellectual lineage of *salonnières* of times past, we present to a handpicked audience a dozen or so specimens from our collection of geniuses. Some of our creative spirits are artists from our circle of acquaintances here in Berlin, others are artists who happened to be passing through Berlin or artists we have flown in especially.'

Mutzek is the forgotten predecessor of the new, much-hyped and somewhat staid Berlin salons of later years. Mutzek was one of the cradles of Mitte's new culture. It offered a blend of experimental music and pop, art, literature and performance for the pleasure of those lucky enough to be there.

Partying is another element of Hakim Bey's TAZ concept. He opens his book with a quote from Nietzsche's last letter to Cosima Wagner: 'However, I now come as Dionysus victorious, who will prepare a great festival on Earth ... Not as though I had much time.' Bey jogs his readers' memories about the utopian socialist Charles Fourier, who denounced the neglect of the senses and introduced the practice of gastrosophy. This exquisitely French art form involved savouring culinary delights and ageing pleasurably. Bey finds yet another supporting source for his theory of festivities in Stephen Pearl Andrews, who, in the nineteenth century, regarded the dinner party as the harbinger of a liberated society. It was a place where all authoritarian structures were dissolved in jovial and festive conviviality. Andrews was *The Communist Manifesto*'s first publisher in the United States, though personally he had no issue with the principle of waged work. He optimistically presaged a world from which all forms of tyranny would have been banished and where every form of freedom would be revered. He wrote that no one would any longer be ashamed to believe in free love. For Andrews, the dinner party was the seed of a new society forming inside the husk of the old one.

In *T.A.Z.*, Bey develops this idea further, declaring the Harlem rent parties of the twenties, the hippies' tribal gatherings of the sixties, nightclubs and anarchist picnics to be liberated zones: 'The party is always "open" because it is not "ordered"; it may be planned, but unless it "happens" it's a failure. The element of spontaneity is crucial ' He proposes a simple definition of a party: 'The essence of the party: face to-face, a group of humans synergize their efforts to realize mutual desires, whether for good food or cheer, dance, conversation, the arts of life; perhaps even for erotic pleasure or to create a communal artwork.'

A party's potential to make people happy was on display every single night in East Berlin. Abandoned rooms were used for living together, dancing, chatting, drinking, smoking, getting high and making music and art.

Robert Lippok can clearly remember the squat in Invalidenstrasse with Mutzek on the ground floor. He comes from a Catholic East Berlin family; his grandfather lived on Zionskirchplatz and his brother still lives there now. Ronald and Robert Lippok played in an experimental band called Ornament & Verbrechen alongside a constantly changing line-up of other musicians. In the mid-nineties Robert, his brother and the bassist Stefan Schneider formed the band To Rococo Rot after meeting at Mutzek in Invalidenstrasse. The house was an anarchic entity.

'It's a shame no one took any pictures of people's flats', Robert Lippok says. 'There were so many crazy interiors. In Invalidenstrasse they did what the people in the Eimer did: they bust through the ceilings and made passageways between rooms. A friend of mine used to live there, an architect from South Africa. He was very quiet and gentlemanly and could draw like a god. He took every drug he could get his hands on and looked like a colonial sugar merchant. He was how I imagined Rimbaud during his African period. Growing up in East Berlin, I heard lots of horror stories. A few churches still had coffins in their crypts, and it turned out that teenagers would drag them outside to scare people.'

Robert Lippok's architect friend pulled something out of an old zinc coffin from the crypt of the Parochialkirche or some other church. 'In his living room there was this box with half a mummy in it – the top half of a dead person. He also hung up some of the mummified cats people often found in attics on his walls.'

In normal times, church catacombs are closed, and the dead rest in their sarcophagi. In Mitte, on the other hand, even corpses were briefly incorporated into daily life and shared rooms with the living. There was a carnival spirit, the world turned upside down.

But a mummy in the living room wasn't the only reminder of the deaths and destruction wreaked on the city. Step outside, and there were reminders all around. East Berlin was full of remains. Every stroll through the streets took you past ruins, vacant sites and faded signs advertising products and shops that had vanished fifty years previously, their owners long since dead. The sediment of bygone times heightened the sensation among residents, old and new, that the present upheaval could not be categorized. Awareness of this transience intensified the present while making you even more acutely aware of the past.

The buried past

On 7 July 1989 Thorsten Schilling has his East German citizenship revoked. Returning to Berlin from a trip to see his parents in Dresden, he finds a summons in his letterbox. He is to present himself at 12 noon that same day, a Friday, to the internal affairs office of Friedrichshain district council.

'I wondered what it might be about, thinking either they're going to really lay into you or they're going to let you leave the country. They'd turned me down a second time shortly before. I'd already been subjected to their Kafkaesque tricks.'

A blonde woman is waiting for Thorsten when he enters Friedrichshain council offices at noon. 'It was called the district council at the time, meaning it was the district soviet.'

The blonde woman doesn't mince her words. 'Herr Schilling, you must leave the GDR by four o'clock this afternoon or you'll be in trouble.' Behind her is a small pile of blue identity cards: Thorsten Schilling is not the first to be kicked out of the country around that time. What came to be known as the Wende was an individual moment in which everything got out of hand, the instant when a person's life took a sudden and unexpected turn and everything changed for ever.

The cause of all these sudden banishments is that Friday's planned demonstration by opposition groups against the rigged local elections of 7 May 1989. Protests have been held on Alexanderplatz every seventh of the month since. Having suspected before the elections that the results would be manipulated, the opposition decides to conduct its own analysis of the outcome.

'We went into the polling stations and wrote down the results during the public count', Thorsten remembers. The results from a good 230 polling stations are compiled on the premises of the Kirche von Unten [Grassroots Church] next to the Elisabethkirche in Berlin-Mitte, then tallied on a computer provided by a Protestant congregation in West Berlin.

Western reporters and diplomats are invited to the election party in the Elisabethkirche's community hall on 7 May 1989. Two days later the West German journalist Karl-Heinz Baum writes about the Kirche von Unten's election observers in the *Frankfurter Rundschau*: 'These "unbidden helpers" are crammed into East Berlin's Elisabethkirche on Sunday evening as the vicar, Thomas Krüger, leads prayers based on the words of the prophet Jeremiah. Jeremiah summoned people to act in order to avoid a calamity for an entire country, Krüger says. It was all about actions and getting involved in the right way. This vote count, Krüger claims, was another step along the path of active involvement.'

Krüger trained as a plastics and elastics production technician in Fürstenwalde before studying Protestant theology. Now a vicar, he is one of the leaders of the Kirche von Unten. Around one hundred people have gathered in the community hall to record the discrepancies between the official and the actual election results, while the votes from the various individual polling stations are totted up in a side room. After a while Thomas Krüger announces the early trends: the number of dissenting votes in some polling stations is between 3 and 20 per cent.

That evening the election observers watch the presentation by Egon Krenz, the head of the central election committee and SED general secretary Erich Honecker's right-hand man, on East German television.

'Egon Krenz's announcement after the polling stations had closed that 98.8 per cent of the votes cast had been cast for the government was a sign. To dip below 99 per cent was a concession', Thorsten Schilling says, 'but it was also clear electoral fraud. We'd counted around 90 per cent of the votes in favour in Berlin. That statistically significant discrepancy with the official results gave us mathematical proof that they'd rigged the results.'

Many voters petition the government in the following days, and some report Egon Krenz to the authorities. The citizens of East Germany learn about the electoral fraud on West German TV.

Thorsten Schilling and Thomas Krüger make a statement to the West German current affairs programme *Kennzeichen D* from Schilling's flat in Friedrichshain. 'Much of it is in the subjunctive: "If it is true that . . . " In my memory of it, I was far braver and spoke in the indicative. I only noticed later while watching the archive footage. You could obviously end up in jail for doing something like that, but we felt we'd had enough.'

While leading prayers at the Elisabethkirche, Krüger signals that getting involved in events could carry personal risk: 'If you jump over the ditch, you have to realize you might fall flat on your back.' Yet getting involved could also be fun, a game of cat and mouse.

Karl-Heinz Baum ends his article by quoting Krüger: 'He warns that it is only proper involvement in society that will demonstrate that "History is not made by laws but founded on differences."'

History is also being made in the community hall. The campaign to publicize the election results is part of a revolutionary movement that aims to break the social stagnation. The church alongside the hall is in some ways a symbol of this stagnation: the Elisabethkirche is a ruin. Grasses, bushes and staghorn sumac are sprouting in the sunlit nave, on top of the porch and outside the portal. In the centre of late-twentieth-century Berlin, this church is like a vestige of a vanished culture, an overgrown temple waiting for intrepid explorers to discover it.

One or two years after the fall of the Wall I was invited to a birthday party in the ruins of the Elisabethkirche. We climbed over the fence, then ate and drank in the weed-choked church by candlelight. I now live only a block away. I didn't often use to think of that picnic in the ruins when I passed the church; the surroundings had changed so much it might just as well have taken place somewhere completely different. After that conversation with Thorsten Schilling, though, my own memories of parties I'd attended in the community hall mingled with the story of that 1989 election party. Now, whenever I walk past, I think of Ingrid and Ruth Kropidlowski.

The Elisabethkirche was built 'in the antique style' by Karl Friedrich Schinkel in 1835. Six Doric columns support the portico, which bears the inscription 'The word of the Lord endures forever.' The church was lavishly renovated in 1935 to mark its centenary. It cost a lot of money, but the parish boasted excellent connections to the new regime. Since the late nineteenth century, anti-Semitic, anti-liberal and anti-democratic forces had been seeking to bring the traditionally liberal Protestant congregations in Rosenthaler Vorstadt under their influence. By 1935 they controlled not only the parish of the Elisabethkirche but also most of the regional Protestant churches. The Deutsche Christen held a majority over members of the Bekennende Kirche [Confessing Church] on the parish council. These 'German Christians', the Nazi organization within the Protestant Church, rejected the Old Testament as 'un-German'. They regarded the baptism of Jews as 'the gateway for foreign blood to enter the body of our nation' and 'a grave danger to our race'. These Nazi Christians zealously excluded Christians with a Jewish background from their parishes. In the centenary year, the parish council voted to outlaw 'Jewish baptisms'. This practice became official church policy four years later in 1939 when the Consistorium, the administrative body of the regional Protestant Church, instructed vicars that the Jewish missionary service alone was authorized to baptise Jews.

The Gesellschaft zur Beförderung des Christentums unter den Juden [Society for Promoting Christianity Among the Jews] had its headquarters in the Messiah chapel of the Segenskirche at Kastanienallee 22. Otto Mähl, the parish's then vicar, protested in 1938 against having to note Jews' prior religion when recording their baptisms, as a state directive required, noting: 'We must answer the question of the person's denomination, not the question of their race.'

Other Protestant vicars scoured the church registers, however. The Berlin-based vicar Karl Themel reported to the Reichsstelle für Sippenforschung [Genealogical Office of the Reich] 2,612 cases of Jews who had converted to the Protestant faith. In 1941 the missionary service was banned and the Messiah chapel sealed off by the Gestapo. This created a problem for the regional church: the Consistorium's theologians wondered who should be responsible in future for baptising 'non Aryans'.

'As things stand, it is probably best to wait and see whether the whole question is not rendered irrelevant by the ongoing deportation of the Jews', reads a handwritten comment in the records.

And so the Elisabethkirche's two vicars refused to christen Ingrid Kropidlowski, who lived with her family at Strelitzer Strasse 25, only a hundred metres from the church. Instead, she received the sacrament in March 1941 from Reverend Kittlaus of the adjoining Chapel of Reconciliation.

Ingrid's mother Ruth came from the Jewish Jacoby family, and Ruth's 'Aryan' husband, the automobile electrician Ferdinand Kropidlowski, became a member of the Jewish community after their wedding. Their daughter Ingrid was initially brought up in accordance with Jewish custom, but in 1939 Ferdinand left the Jewish community to revert to the Protestant faith, soon followed by his wife Ruth. For a year Ingrid was allowed to attend the special class for Christian children of Jewish origin at the First Jewish Primary School in Kaiserstrasse near Alexanderplatz. In the summer of 1942, however, she was officially categorized as a Jew and banned from continuing at the school. The status of 'first-degree Mischling', which protected some people from deportation and murder, was only granted to those who 'did not incline to Judaism', which meant that they didn't belong to the Jewish community, and had been both baptised and brought up as Christians. The baptism must have taken place before the passing of the Reichsbürgergesetz [Law of Citizens of the Reich]. Ingrid's father died in suspicious circumstances in 1942. On 17 June 1943 eight-year-old Ingrid and her mother Ruth were deported to Terezin.

A little under two years later, on the night of 8–9 March 1945, phosphorous firebombs fell from the sky, hitting the Elisabethkirche but leaving the adjacent community hall unscathed. The church was gutted, its ruins a permanent reminder that something once occurred here, although it discloses no details.

After the Wall came down, the bullet holes in the facades and the vacant plots all over Mitte were reminders of the war, but virtually nothing commemorated the persecution of the many Jews who lived in the area up to 1943.

Following Thomas Krüger's prayer in the community hall next to the Elisabethkirche, twenty years passed before the church was substantially repaired and the regional Protestant Church's 'Working Group on Christians of Jewish Origin under National Socialism' set about investigating the circumstances of the denial of baptism to Ingrid Kropidlowski. Remembrance Stolpersteine (literally, 'stumbling stones'; metaphorically, 'stumbling blocks') were laid for Ingrid and Ruth Kroplidowski outside their last known address in Strelitzer Strasse, but they reveal nothing about their connections to the Elisabethkirche. There is now a plaque outside the church with information about the activities of the Kirche von Unten.

The East German state was eager to forget Mitte's Nazi past. It created a new centre around Alexanderplatz, and from then on, the television tower stood guard in the night over the crumbling houses of the Spandauer, Rosenthaler and Oranienburger areas.

A good ten years before the fall of the Wall, Eike Geisel travels to the East German capital and wanders around the neighbourhood on the edge of Alexanderplatz. Focusing on the streets to the east of Alte Schönhauser Strasse, he is interested in the Jewish immigrants who once lived here among the barns, stables and storage sheds that had been banished to outside the city gates. In his book *Im Scheunenviertel* [*In the Barn Quarter*], a collection of historical documents, memoirs and photographs published in 1981, Geisel writes that these outhouses gave the neighbourhood its name. Some of the streets and alleys, where livestock was kept in backyards, had the ramshackle look of a village that had survived within the city. Rapid population growth around the turn of the twentieth century fuelled a boom in land prices in the centre of Berlin.

'The owners pin their hopes of making a profit on the crumbling facades, and the unheatable houses fire up land prices',

Geisel writes. Speculators allowed the Scheunenviertel to decay in anticipation of being able to demolish the buildings one day and sell the now lucrative land. Until that time, the greatest profit was to be made by collecting rent but making no investment in the houses themselves. Geisel drily remarks that a Wall had now dashed these hopes, bringing an end to the speculation.

There was a steady influx of Eastern European Jews from the end of the nineteenth century, and several thousand once lived in this densely populated neighbourhood. Even larger numbers ended up stranded here after the First World War, either because Berlin was at least better than their home, or because they hadn't made it to America. By the end of the 1970s, however, there was no trace of their existence in the Scheunenviertel. The area between Münzstrasse and Linienstrasse divulges its past only to those already familiar with it, Geisel writes.

'There is nothing left, other than the squalor of the buildings. Every street in the neighbourhood is like an unattractive jaw full of gaps, every house a welfare case made of stone. Every house front is a grey, gaping portal offering no glimpse of the past', he adds. These buildings have nothing to say to him. 'There was once a story, but there is no story now. The objects have nothing left to tell.' He believes that the Nazis were the secret victors of the era. 'If whatever might have stood as a reminder to them had disappeared, then the murdered were worse than dead – they had never lived.' What Geisel does not mention is that the Wall helped to create the space in which this forgetting was coordinated.

In Grenadierstrasse (renamed Almstadtstrasse in the GDR) Geisel finds a 'last, shocking remnant' of the former Jewish community – three Hebrew letters spelling the word 'kosher'. He reads them as a warning about memory loss, as a 'weird relic, not erased like those to whom it was an unmistakable symbol of their difference', and prophesies that 'it will be plastered over and smeared with weatherproof paint'. What remains will be tidily renovated 'so that the fissured monuments that represent anthropology after Auschwitz, and the generalized loss of memory, lose their last, diffuse capacity to upset people'.

Only three years after the publication of Geisel's book, his prediction came true. Workers from Gera erected tidy prefabricated blocks equipped with running hot water in the gaps in the Scheunenviertel. They also refurbished some of the old buildings. One day, it was the turn of the house at Almstadtstrasse 18. It was painted a synthetic cream colour. East German academics and artists also preferred spacious old apartments to the cramped rooms of the tower blocks. The intelligentsia in West and East alike were discovering the inner cities, and in East Berlin they moved to Prenzlauer Berg or the Scheunenviertel, the former slum on the fringes of Alexanderplatz.

Around the same time as Eike Geisel was investigating the Scheunenviertel, the East Berlin author Irina Liebmann was photographing the streets around Hackescher Markt as part of her research for a novel set in the area between Friedrichstrasse and Alexanderplatz.

'It was the only place where there was still a decent bit of the old city centre. Not a tourist area like now – more of an attic cluttered with furniture from Berlin's days as a cosmopolitan city', she writes in the foreword to her book of photographs, which came out in 2002. In her pictures the streets have been swept clean, the facades are weathered and grey, and often the plaster has fallen off. Buildings alternate with vacant plots, some of which are buried to varying depths in bricks and rubble from demolished houses. As she

explored the area, she detected a whiff of adventure and dis-
order, a promising sign 'in a country where individualism
never really stood a chance'. There were traces of luxury,
'even if it was no more than a decommissioned lift or a green
glazed tile in the staircase'.

Irina Liebmann discovered the vestiges of a time when
variety ruled. What she found more surprising, though, was
that the neighbourhood's residents in the 1980s knew little
or nothing about the people who had lived here before them.
She saw telephone numbers of long-vanished companies
painted on firewalls and Stars of David woven into staircase ornamentation. She interviewed old women who had
lived in these streets their whole lives. Most of them were
poor, living in dingy, poorly heated flats and boiling potatoes for lunch. They talked about the former proprietors of
the shops that had been shuttered for decades and about the
prostitutes in Mulackstrasse who earned a good living from
their customers up to a ripe old age. The old women in the
neighbourhood were happy to give Irina Liebmann information. Until, that is, she asked about families who had ceased
to live here long ago.

'One woman, for instance, saw children at the window of
the house opposite in the winter of 1943. Their parents must
have been arrested and never came home again, and the
small children were glued to the glass like flies, scrabbling
up and down the panes. They must have been locked in and
dying of thirst, such little children. She told this story several
times, with warmth and compassion.'

However, the next time the author came round, the doors
remained steadfastly shut.

The state of the workers and farmers was committed to
anti-fascism. National Socialism appeared to have happened elsewhere. The GDR's propaganda presented the
Federal Republic of Germany as the successor state of the

Third Reich, its cultural life dominated by a host of former Nazis firmly ensconced in the upper echelons of business, civil service and politics. What's more, the BRD, as the East Germans liked to abbreviate the Bundesrepublik Deutschland, was seen as a hotbed of neo-fascist machinations. The fact that many National Socialists had turned socialist in 1945 and enjoyed government or party careers in East Germany didn't correspond to the GDR's image of itself. In the context of the Cold War, the comrades in the SED didn't think it wise to precipitate a debate about the country's Nazi past. By definition the Nazis were in the BRD, while the GDR was home only to resistance fighters and anti-fascists. There were no ex-Nazis in East Germany – and in a sense there were no more Jews there either.

'I've read many, many Jewish authors of all kinds, from Marxists through to conservatives. I didn't really have a clear idea of what Jewishness meant, but it has always interested me', the writer Chaim Noll recalls. 'I had to assert that interest against outside resistance. They tried to persuade me that there was no such thing as Jewish thought, that it didn't exist in East Germany. A few books by Yiddish popular writers from Eastern Europe were published in East Germany and naturally the works of Arnold Zweig, Anna Seghers, Friedrich Wolf and that lot. They were born Jewish, but now they were socialist writers. My father always saw himself as a socialist writer too. The persecution of "Zionist societies" and "activities" in the early years of the GDR intimidated many Jewish intellectuals and drove them to deny their Jewish roots. Until 1987 there were no Jewish rabbis and no *mohel*, and they made it hard to perform the essential rituals of Jewish life such as circumcision and bar mitzvahs. If there was a Jewish wedding – and I know of only one – a rabbi was brought in from abroad. The politically correct way to write about Jews in East Germany was to portray them as victims of the Nazis, so it was an act of revolt even to explore your identity as a Jew.'

References to brave communist resistance fighters became a screen memory for a society that refused to acknowledge that many people in East Berlin, Dresden, Leipzig, Magdeburg and Rostock had eagerly gone along with the Nazis. The resulting climate of persistent denial fostered a neo-Nazi subculture. Racist and anti-Semitic incidents had been on the rise since the 1970s, and the Stasi was well aware of this fact. It concluded in 1986 that fascist comments had increased 'in number and significance'. A few severe sentences were handed down. Some 1,000 violent, extreme right-wing skinheads were known to the authorities, but there was no public debate about the problem. It was only when thirty skinheads stormed the Zionskirche in 1987 at the end of a gig by the West Berlin band Element of Crime and beat up some of the 2,000-strong crowd that the subject of neo-Nazis could no longer be swept under the carpet. Groups of punks fought back, and several people were injured. The police and the Stasi had observed the attack but refused to intervene when the skinheads shouted 'Sieg Heil!' and 'No Jews in German churches!' It took some time for the ringleaders to be arrested and sentenced to prison terms.

When the Wall fell, neo-Nazis had also become active in Mitte and Prenzlauer Berg, where a right-wing subculture was seeking to gain a foothold. People out on the streets late at night would sometimes switch pavement, just to be on the safe side. It was better not to linger around places like Lichtenberg railway station on your own. East Berlin's left-wing squatters made a security pact with the police to protect themselves from roving gangs of neo-Nazis. The police officers gave the squatters tips about building barricades. In summer 1990 neo-Nazis attacked Art House Tacheles in Oranienburger Strasse, hurling a Molotov cocktail in one squatter's face. In the cellar of an occupied house in Kastanienallee they ripped open a gas pipe, set fire to it and daubed swastikas on the walls. The neo-Nazis of East Berlin represented the return of the suppressed past in physical form.

In the post-reunification years there were pogroms and arson attacks in Hoyerswerda and Rostock in the old East, Mölln and Solingen in former West Germany. The racist mob was anarchy's most sinister manifestation. People witnessed the events in Rostock-Lichtenhagen in 1992 on their television sets, and Germany looked on as if what was unfolding on this council estate might not be completely normal, but was still a natural process somehow. As if the only option were to stand there and record what was happening. Everyone watched on as the mob built up and up over several days and eventually began to attack people who had applied for asylum in Germany. The state had left the asylum seekers camping outside with children and babies and had not provided them with sufficient numbers of showers and toilets, forcing them to relieve themselves below the balconies of the housing blocks.

Neo-Nazis came agitating, and at some stage one of them set fire to a block housing Vietnamese people to whom the mob contemptuously referred as 'Fijis'. The residents were able to escape at the very last moment across the rooftop. Whereas the police would respond to the slightest indication of a riot in Hamburg or Berlin by sending in units of battle-hardened officers, here in Rostock they pulled back and watched the situation unfold. TV crews were there filming the scenes, and so Germany's first post-war pogrom was broadcast live on public television. 'A staged disaster' serving a political purpose, one critical observer remarked twenty years after the event. The asylum laws were amended soon afterwards.

In Berlin, Antifa did its best to drive neo-Nazi activity back into the outskirts, as extreme right-wing cadres of the subsequently banned Freiheitliche Deutsche Arbeiterpartei [the Free German Workers' Party] had infiltrated even the bohemian district of Prenzlauer Berg. The squatter-artist-bohemian counterculture of Berlin-Mitte might have carried on partying, but its more alert members did so with an awareness of the area's history.

'I never saw the scene as purely hedonistic', says Christoph Heller. 'We knew exactly what was at stake. People from West and East alike were highly influenced by their Cold War education. We'd grown up with the two systems. It wasn't this sudden liberation, like, "Wow, the Wall's down! The deutschmark's here!" Instead, all of a sudden, the whole of history, up to and including the Nazi period, was exposed and made visible.'

The real issue, though, was whether people would take the time to look and ask themselves how things used to be.

The disappearance of all memory of the deported, so deplored by Eike Geisel, came to an end in Berlin when the artist Gunter Demnig laid the first of his fifty-one Stolpersteine in Oranienstrasse in Kreuzberg in May 1996 – without official permission. Since then, their number has grown to over 8,500. The 10-cm-square brass plates commemorate those deported and murdered by the Nazis outside their former homes. Now you could read the names of whole families in front of some houses in Mitte, while, at the same time, the facades in the eastern half of the city were being restored and the empty sites developed. First it was people who disappeared from Mitte, then the bomb damage and the bullet holes, and finally the Stolpersteine made even those disappearances disappear. Representation – which is what the decentralized Stolperstein memorials are – always establishes a distance from events. The more colourful and 'authentic' that presentations of the Second World War and National Socialism have become in recent decades, through eyewitness accounts, photographs, documentary films, biopics and feature films, the more thoroughly the actual traces of that time have been purged from our daily lives. The vacant plots gave way to buildings, the gaps caused by bombs were filled in, and the marks machine-gunners left in the walls of Mitte, so ubiquitous in the nineties, have been practically erased. Sometimes, historicization and forgetting are merely variations of the same process.

'Where are the cripples that helped us as children to understand what it means to lose the war? They can only be seen in cemeteries now', run the lyrics of a song recorded by the Dusseldorf punk band Family 5 a few years before the Wall came down. We could rewrite that song for 1990s Berlin like this: 'Where are the vacant plots gone that helped us as ravers to understand what it means to lose the war? They can only be seen in photos now.'

The GDR is like a predigital Facebook

When Thorsten Schilling looks out of his Berlin office window today, he sees the old Checkpoint Charlie border crossing in Friedrichstrasse. He works in a new building erected after the Wende on the former East German side of the Wall. Thorsten is head of the multimedia department of the Federal Agency for Civic Education. He was born in Dresden and still speaks German with a slight Saxon brogue. He moved from Leipzig to Berlin in 1986 after four years studying Marxist-Leninist philosophy at Karl Marx University in Leipzig. He was destined to become a university lecturer in Marxism-Leninism to teach students the historical truth.

'I was one of only a few – maybe five or six out of 120 students – who weren't in the Party, but I was a top student, which means that I got a First in every exam apart from one. I even won a scholarship. But I was told: "You're not in the Party? That won't do." I tried to wriggle out of it, but as a Catholic theology student you can't just say, "Nuh, I'm not really into God, I'm not going to be a priest anyway." It was a slightly schizophrenic situation from the start.'

In 1985 Mikhail Sergeyevich Gorbachev became General Secretary of the Central Committee of the Communist Party of the Soviet Union. He had first-hand knowledge of the West from several visits. At the 27th Congress of the CPSU, barely a year after taking office, Gorbachev, who later described himself as a social democrat, introduced a series of reforms he branded 'glasnost' and 'perestroika' – transparency and restructuring. A few months later, in East Germany, the SED held its annual congress.

'People were wondering if they were going to swing in behind Gorbachev's perestroika policy or not', Thorsten Schilling recalls.

It became clear that they wouldn't when the SED's chief ideologue, Kurt Hager, asked his interviewers from the West German news magazine *Stern*: 'If your neighbour were to change the wallpaper in his flat, would you feel obliged to hang new wallpaper in your own?' In East Germany this earned Hager the nickname of 'Tapeten-Kutte' ('Wallpaper Kurt'). His interview stressed the GDR's utter disinterest in opening up, and perestroika was now the Politburo's bogeyman. Erich Honecker criticized Gorbachev's lack of commitment to class war and came to the conclusion, given developments in the rest of the Eastern Bloc, that only in East Germany were socialist values still fully ingrained in the people.

'Until that point the motto had always been "learning from the Soviet Union means learning to win." By the late eighties we had the feeling that things were unwinding but that it might still take a long time. Honecker and the others were seventy – they might hang around for another ten years or more. That's an eternity when you're in your mid-twenties. At the same time, though, there was this sense of "Why fight something that's already done for?"'

Only by recalling the weariness that preceded it can we understand many East German citizens' excitement when the Wall fell, as well as the actions of opposition figures who accepted positions of responsibility in government and administration. Thorsten Schilling describes the experience of young people growing up in a society whose end can already be smelled and felt.

The author Chaim Noll, who is six years older than Thorsten, has similar memories of the final years of the GDR 'We were living in a decaying society that wasn't allowed to be seen as such. Officially, it was a progressive and flourishing socialist society. The picture it projected of itself remained upbeat to the very end. East Germany had been bankrupt since the seventies, and yet they continued to claim that the plan had been more than fulfilled.'

A phrase Erich Honecker proclaimed to the workers of a microelectronics enterprise in Erfurt later became famous: 'It takes more than an ox or a donkey to get in the way of socialist victory!'

Chaim sees the absurdity of this split between the regime's self-representation and reality. In contrast to many others, he sensed even in the early eighties that he was living in a decadent society. 'Until the summer of 1989, a lot of people, including many in the West, believed that it would carry on that way forever.' Chaim is convinced that, had it not been for all the funding from the West, the system would have collapsed earlier. 'The monetary payments from Kohl's West German government kept the regime unnecessarily on life support.'

The author predicted the end of the East German state in his novel *Der goldene Löffel* [*The Golden Spoon*], which was published in West Germany in September 1989. It tells the story of Adam, the son of an intellectual loyal to the Party. Many of Adam's friends also have parents in important positions in the Party and in government. His friend Markus's father is a journalist who hasn't written anything for years. He drinks instead, and eventually throws himself out of his office window. Journalists did repeatedly leap to their deaths from the offices of the *Berliner Zeitung* newspaper on Alexanderplatz, gaining the building the sarcastic name of 'Springer-Hochhaus' ['high-jump high-rise'[2]].

Adam and his friends are increasingly cynical about their parents and a state whose initials suggest it is a socialist democracy, but which is actually a totalitarian system. Not yet twenty, Adam has internalized the need to be wary of every word.

Adam's story bears many similarities to its author's. Chaim was born into a communist family with Jewish roots in Berlin in 1954 as Hans Noll. His father, Dieter Noll, was the author of a novel that was successful in the GDR and beyond, as well as a member of the socialist nomenklatura. Chaim disowned his father when Dieter described authors critical of the system as 'broken people'. Allowed to emigrate to the West in 1984, Chaim and his family lived first in West Berlin and then in Rome. The Nolls eventually moved to Israel, where Chaim now lives in a small town near Be'er Sheva.

---

[2] Springer ('jumper') is also the name of a West German multinational publishing company.

Chaim Noll qualifies his novels as an attempt to paint a psychologically credible portrait of what happened to people in East Germany. 'Everyone, from top to bottom, no matter his or her social class, fell victim to this system. There was huge pressure to perform in the GDR. This whole thing no longer worked and assumed ever more inhumane traits.' In Noll's novel the German socialists seem to have a pathological obsession with order. 'East German socialism was particularly oppressive, and this was accentuated in comparison with other Eastern Bloc countries by a certain complicity, a moral cowardice, a narrow-mindedness. We went to Poland or Hungary for a breath of fresh air because there were occasional dissenting voices there, whereas East Germany was more or less intellectually barren. That changed later with the civil rights activists, and it burst apart in the 1980s. The bulk of the population complied with the rules, though. Even as children we suffered greatly from the whole GDR mentality. The climate was incredibly petty, a negativity that went hand in glove with the brutality directed at anyone who didn't fit the mould. Basically, everything was forbidden.'

At school he saw teenagers expelled from extended secondary school and banned from taking their final exams because they had a beard or long hair or wore clothes deemed provocative. 'In the 1950s it was stripy socks, later it was parkas. Lives were destroyed over insignificant details like these, all because someone breached one or other of the regime's dress codes.'

If you moved to East Berlin in 1990, you got a good sense of what it must have been like. You'd entered a territory patrolled by small-minded pensioners outraged by any tiny transgression, even crossing the road when the pedestrian light was red. This was clearly a country where punishment and order were all-pervasive to the end.

When Chaim Noll swapped East Germany for West Berlin, Thorsten Schilling was still studying at Karl Marx University, but he was also part of Leipzig's bohemian scene. He lived in an apartment on Körnerplatz where he and his flatmate Gerd Harry Lybke, aka 'Judy', exhibited work by young artists. Lybke would later continue what began as a hobby with his Galerie Eigen + Art.

After the Wende, Lybke moved his gallery to premises on Auguststrasse in Berlin-Mitte, halfway between Tacheles and the Eimer. He was subsequently instrumental in establishing the paintings of Neo Rauch, and with him the so-called New Leipzig School, on the US art market.

'I had one foot in the establishment and one outside', Thorsten remembers. 'It reached the point, though, where it became impossible to continue my studies. I'd read too much French post-structuralist theory. I could no longer even pretend to reconcile that with Marxist-Leninist discourse. I sent the university a letter telling them I wasn't coming back and saw no point in Marxism-Leninism. It caused a massive scandal. It became known as "the Schilling case". They held a plenary session with a hundred students in the lecture theatre, all incredibly Stalinist, but I didn't attend.'

Thorsten left Leipzig and moved to East Berlin. The city seemed harder to penetrate than the more manageably sized Leipzig.

'As it turned out, though, after a while you knew everyone', he says. 'If you had the right attitude, it wasn't hard to make friends. There were a few loosely connected groups of ten, twenty or thirty people.'

One of the places where people met up was at the weekly jazz evening at the Haus der Jungen Talente every Monday. It was where Wolle Neugebauer and his mates threw their Tekknozid parties after the fall of the Wall. For a time, Thorsten went at least once a week to see a play at the

Deutsches Theater, and there were parties and discussions in the theatre cafeteria afterwards. The theatre's technicians included some of East Berlin's first punks.

'I think it was the literary theorist Hans Ulrich Gumbrecht who said that East Germany was an oral culture', he remarks. 'I think that's true. Basically, it was like a predigital Facebook.' Thorsten himself is the best possible proof of Gumbrecht's theory. History comes to life as he tells it. 'You would just go round and see people. If they weren't in, you'd stick a message on the door and come back the next day. You knew people would usually be hanging out in some pub or other.'

Most flats in East Berlin didn't have a telephone, and that remained the case many years after the Wall came down. Long queues formed outside public phone boxes. People dropped in on one another and left notes on the pads hanging on the doors, just as East Berliners did before the Wende. If you wanted to meet up with someone, you went to a bar like the Friseur. Post-Wende society was also an oral culture, and its means of communications included graffiti and flyers. Some were invitations to parties in a cellar somewhere; others were calls to demonstrate, for example the graffito on an end wall in Senefelder Platz that read 'Demo here 5 pm' with a painted arrow pointing to the square. If you wanted to know where to go in the evening, you just had to talk to people; there was no app to show the way.

Before the fall of the Wall, East German counterculture was mainly based on word of mouth and small get-togethers.

'That way of meeting and making arrangements gave rise to a milieu of artists, scientists and editors – a bohemian society in the widest possible sense of the word', Thorsten Schilling says of the time before the Wende. 'Yeah, bohemian is a romantic term.' It is a fitting description of Thorsten's financial circumstances. He earned his living from making lampshades out of string and selling them on the black market, in the street or at the market. 'I did that once a week and could live comfortably on the income. It didn't cost that much to get by, really.'

By the summer of 1986, the works of Foucault, Derrida and other post-structuralist and postmodern thinkers were also beginning to circulate in East Germany.

'Postmodernism came to the East quite late. It's clear from samizdat[3] writings that the Prenzlauer Berg scene, including Stasi people like Rainer Schedliniski[4] and Sascha Anderson,[5] were rehashing Foucault and Baudrillard.' Thorsten believes that this caused problems for the cultural opposition. 'Because of the cultural relativism ingrained in postmodern theory, the countermovement became infected with the same cynicism the state demonstrated towards its people. It put too much emphasis on the cultural symbolic code.'

In his student days Thorsten had read the simulation theory of Jean Baudrillard, the French philosopher and translator of Karl Marx. Thorsten recognized Baudrillard's notion of the world as simulacrum in the GDR, even though the French philosopher originally applied it to capitalism.

'There was simulation everywhere, but it was a gory simulation, culminating in the Stasi prison in Hohenschönhausen. People were murdered, destroyed and brought to their knees.

---

[3] Samizdat (Russian for 'self-publishing') was a means by which dissidents in the former Eastern Bloc reproduced censored and underground publications and passed them from reader to reader.

[4] Rainer Schedlinski (1956–2019) was a German poet and essayist. A leading dissident author in East Germany in the 1980s, he was later revealed to have worked for the Stasi as an informer.

[5] Sascha Anderson (b. 1953) is a German writer and artist who played a major role in the alternative scene in 1980s East Berlin, despite having been recruited as a Stasi informer in 1975 under the code name 'Fritz Müller'.

Imprisoned dissidents were secretly subjected to radioactive irradiation. We only found out some of those things later. But the feeling that it was not just a game of symbols but a bloody game with bodies too – that feeling was always present. The feeling that your life might be at stake.' Thorsten views 1980s East Germany as the scene of a kind of black postmodernism: 'Black as in: it can be fatal, it can be absolutely brutal. Utterly cynical and at the same time powerless. Unintentionally weird.'

Thorsten and his friends invented campaigns riffing on this cynicism. 'We put a poem printed in *Neues Deutschland* to music: "With coltsfoot, lettuce and broom / Let socialism bloom!" That was on the second page of the country's leading newspaper, and you can only think: These people are nuts! Krüger and a few more of us put together a performance for a youth club in Treptow, and we suggested doing a skit about the GDR.' Thorsten and his mates recited poems from the socialist canon by people like Kurt Bartel (KuBa), the Party poet laureate who died in 1967, and sang pioneer songs.

They would meet up every Thursday at the home of a doctor they knew who could get hold of Hungarian wine. 'Thomas Krüger was often there. He studied theology and then trained as a vicar with the Kirche von Unten. Peter Wawerzinek, the poet Matthias Baader Holst and others. On Thursdays, the community radio in West Berlin, Radio 100, broadcast a programme by Frieder Butzmann and Thomas Kapiclski. We would sit there, drinking red wine and crying with laughter at their sketches at the Fischlabor in Schöneberg. They were kindred spirits, we felt. Butzmann and Kapielski were doing the same things as us – exaggerating everything, making it sound totally absurd – but to the symbolic system of the West.'

Unlike in the West, however, it was possible to live a marginal life in East Berlin with no financial pressures, as

Schilling learnt from chatting to visitors from West Berlin. 'We came across as a kind of wild circus to people stressed out by the rat race in the West. They came over and saw all the clapped-out houses. If you were a Westerner and highly sensitive, neurotic and anxious, surrounded by advertising, you'd enter these surroundings and feel shock.'

Thorsten experienced this same feeling twenty years later looking at photos of the period after the Wall came down.

'I realized what people from the West must have seen back then. There's this war-torn landscape, and then people emerge from the ruins and they're weird too. They've read Heidegger and lots of other stuff besides. They're smart. Matthias Baader Holst, for example, was as well-read as any guy you're likely to meet. Before coming to Berlin he'd spent years and years devouring books in Halle university library. He was a walking literary encyclopaedia, but he was of course totally unhinged too. Someone from West Berlin, a middle-class lad – say, someone studying medicine – would just stand there staring with his jaw on the floor.'

Thorsten and his friends took advantage of their new-found exoticism in the eyes of Western tourists in search of the wild Eastern bohemian lifestyle – they got them to smuggle whisky and coveted books across the border.

'We did realize, though, that if the West ever came, it would all be over. We thought to ourselves, "It's shit here, but things are shitty in the West too." We were detached from both, in a way.' Intellectuals in the East were smart enough to know that freedom also has a price.

Friday 7 July 1989 is the day Thorsten finally gets to see the West with his own eyes. After being informed that he has to leave the GDR within a matter of hours, he goes home to look for some passport photos. After that, he makes for a phone box and calls a friend in Kreuzberg to announce, 'I'm coming today. I'll probably be there around three.' Then he returns to the council offices and hands in his East German identity card, receiving in return a one-way visa out of the GDR. He leaves East Germany via the 'Palace of Tears' at Friedrichstrasse station and takes the underground to West Berlin.

'It was a whole different kettle of fish, discovering the West – the forbidden land. It was this crazy, existential sensation. Like watching films about New York for years, and then all of sudden you're there. It was a physical and sensory experience at first. It smelled different, it looked different. You had to learn everything from scratch again. I asked a saleswoman at Kreuzberg market hall, "Have you got any salami?" A typical Easterner's question. "Have you got any?" means "Is there any today?" Obviously, that kind of question is totally inappropriate in the West, where there's too much of everything. The woman replied, "Sure, what kind?" It was this seminal moment when I thought, "OK, this woman knows more about salami than you do."'

The neighbourhood policeman

Thorsten Schilling didn't feel like moving back to East Berlin directly after the Wall opened, so he didn't take part in the first enthusiastic forays across the border by old and new West Berliners.

'That was when people were bagging 140-square-metre flats on Kollwitzplatz for 20 East German marks, the winter of 1990–1 when people in the East were rattled. That carried on until the spring when it became clear that the Volkskammer elections would result in a grand coalition government. The SED was finished. People in the administration were very reticent, and the police suddenly felt intimidated. Often, all it would take was for someone to have a stern word – the way Westerners do. They knew how to go about it, strutting around like the new big chiefs, totally sure of themselves. The officials in the administration behaved very submissively at first because they weren't sure. Are these guys really our new bosses? What's going to happen to me? Don't put a foot wrong. The old bosses were gone, and they didn't know what the new bosses were really like.'

Many people seized the opportunity and moved to areas with nice old buildings like Prenzlauer Berg and Mitte. Flats used to be squatted and converted without permission in the GDR, and there was no outcry. While Thorsten was still studying in Leipzig, he'd occupied a one-room flat at the back of a building in Oderberger Strasse in Prenzlauer Berg. 'No one was even remotely interested until the fire service practised putting out a blaze next door. It was uninhabitable after that, but until then it was my pad in Berlin.'

There was a shortage of housing in West Berlin, and so when the Wall came down many people made the most of what was available in the east of the city, where tens of thousands of apartments had been abandoned. People used to roam through Mitte, Prenzlauer Berg and Friedrichshain, looking for an apartment that was obviously unoccupied.

Christoph Keller was one such opportunist. 'There were absolutely masses of empty apartments. You could just walk in. Kick the door down first, then change the lock and find out the reference of the tenancy agreement. By German law, if you'd paid rent for three months, that entitled you to a rental agreement for that flat', he says.

Susanne and Christina did exactly the same thing, taking over two abandoned one-room flats on the second floor of a house on a back courtyard in Lychener Strasse in Prenzlauer Berg. The two adjoining flats were connected by a hole at eye level, and the two neighbours could climb up on a chair and crawl through the hole if they wanted to. In fact, it turned out to be far more practical to go out of their own front door and in through the other's. They never carried out Christina's plan of connecting the two flats with a communicating door, and the hole stayed where it was – a promise forever dangling before their eyes. This crude chink suggested to the two neighbours that not only could everything in here and out there be different, but it could change *at any moment*; they only had to do it.

For three months Christina and Susanne deposited their rent in an account in the name of KWV. Officially, KWV stood for Kommunale Wohnungsverwaltung [Municipal Housing Department], but it was commonly referred to as Kann Weiter Verfallen ('Leave It to Rot'). The KWV Prenzlauer Berg was soon renamed WIP, Wohnen in Prenzlauer Berg [Living in Prenzlauer Berg]. The two young women had found out the KWV's account number as well as the current rental price per square metre, which, even a few months after the monetary reforms, was still at practically socialist levels.

After paying their rent punctually for three months, Christina and Susanne show up at the desk of the relevant WIP official in Schwedter Strasse one day to formalize their tenancy situation.

The official asks them, 'Why didn't you put your names down on the list of housing applicants like any other citizen?' She grumbles a bit but doesn't seek to obstruct Susanne and Christina's plans any further, and so they leave the office again clutching legitimate rental agreements.

By the time Thorsten thought about moving somewhere on the edge of the old Scheunenviertel, it was no longer so easy to find a flat, let alone an empty building.

'We walked along Mulackstrasse, Grete, me and a few other people. There were all these deserted buildings which the East German government wanted to leave to collapse.'

The state was planning to demolish virtually the whole western part of the old Scheunenviertel between Rosa Luxemburg Strasse and Rosenthaler Strasse to make space for prefabricated blocks. The old buildings in the rest of the neighbourhood north of Oranienburger Strasse had also been deliberately allowed to decay since the war. In the early eighties, the odd new building was inserted here and there on a vacant plot. Even before the Wende, local initiatives campaigned to preserve the built heritage and general character of the streets of the Oranienburger, Rosenthaler and Spandauer areas.

'There was this ruin at the end of Mulackstrasse', Thorsten recalls, 'that contained what was known as a Monday bar, which meant it was open every Monday. It was crazy that,

Fig. 6 View of the backs of the buildings at Kleine Hamburger Strasse 3–5

forty years after the war, there were still so many ruins in the city centre.'

A slogan has been painted across the entire width of the facade of the building at Mulackstrasse 37: 'Nothing left standing by the war will survive socialism.' The windows are unglazed and, in their place, torn plastic sheeting has been hung up behind each window frame. The shutters over the window of a shop that has been closed for ages haven't been pulled down all the way, and the entrance is boarded up from inside. Most of the plaster on the facade is missing. As if in deliberate mockery, a plaque stating that the building is of historical significance has been put up beside the door.

Thorsten and his friends look it over.

'Suddenly this guy comes riding up on a bike. He says, "What are you doing here?" We say, "We're thinking of squatting this place." He stands there, a lanky, slightly deranged-looking guy in his late forties, straddling his bike with sandals on his feet. He introduces himself as Peter, then says, "No way, you can't just move in. This house is already taken." I ask him who he is. He says, "We're this kind of local group," putting on this big Western act. I ask him where he comes from. "I'm an East German now too and I think things need managing a bit differently", he says. He'd appointed himself a local contact person for the fringe movement, a kind of neighbourhood policeman, so he had something to do in life. And he'd hurriedly acquired East German citizenship to give himself some authenticity.'

Peter, this ageing sandal-wearing hippie, obviously has no idea that he is perceived as a representative of the new order, even if that order is the left-wing alternative Kreuzberg scene.

'We knew immediately that he was going to be a thorn in our side', Thorsten says. 'We'd got there too late.'

When he eventually finds a place to live in Alte Schönhauser Strasse, there is only one shop left – a pet shop with nothing but a small aquarium in its window.

Ben de Biel was also immediately attracted to the area. He was in his early twenties when he travelled from Hamburg to Berlin in February 1990 to take photos.

'Looking around, I thought, I'd be a total idiot to stay in Hamburg now. Everything's empty here and it costs nothing. I looked at it in very practical terms. If all goes well, I'll only start paying for electricity and rent in five years' time – and that's exactly how things turned out.'

Six months after his first visit, Ben was back living in a building in Kleine Hamburger Strasse which had only one occupant when the squatters arrived. There was virtually no one in any of the surrounding buildings either.

'The Easterners knew the score. They knew the GDR intended to raze the Scheunenviertel to the ground', Ben says. 'People moved into the houses to forestall the demolition. They could be demolished once all the tenants had moved out, even if nothing was built in their place. So to stop that happening someone would often live on their own in a building. One of the floors in our building was still in good condition, and there was a bathroom too.'

One of his photos shows just what wrecks the buildings on Kleine Hamburger Strasse had become. Some of the flats are occupied, whereas others have been gutted by fire. There's a tree growing on one roof.

The shortage of housing in the West was a good reason to move east, but many people also came because they wanted to experience the city as it changed. Dietrich Boelter had been studying in West Berlin since 1987 and decided to head east when the Wall came down. What he'd heard was that you had to go to WBM, the Wohnungsbaugesellschaft

Berlin-Mitte [Berlin-Mitte Housing Association]. There, they handed him seven keys to flats and gave him the addresses. He was told to come back in a couple of hours and return the keys. One of the flats was in Schröderstrasse.

'It hadn't been renovated, but I walked around the flat and found a small balcony out the back. It had a view of the Zille park. Great, I thought, it's got a park nearby and lots of light.'

That's an important detail because Schröderstrasse was pretty dark and not very welcoming. Only after a few weeks did Dietrich realize that he was living near Invalidenstrasse where there was an old Intershop – one of the East German government-run shops where you had to pay in hard currency. He knew the street from earlier days.

'While the Wall was still there, I often used to drive along Invalidenstrasse, but I had a very different perception of it at the time. The Invalidenstrasse border crossing used to be by the bridge where the Ministry for Economic Affairs is now. My girlfriend and I had met this gay couple in Prenzlauer Berg. We'd bring them tomatoes and fennel from West Berlin, cook together and make sure we were back by twelve.'

When Dietrich moved east, not much had changed yet. All the same, he was there not as a visitor now but as a new arrival, which made a world of difference.

'There were only about four or five people from the West in the whole of Schröderstrasse', he says. He was the only West German in his building. 'The people working in the bakery on the corner never said hello when I bought bread rolls for breakfast. "Why are you so surprised?" my East German neighbour told me. "You're from the West."'

The fall of the Wall radically altered the relationship between West and East. Beforehand, the two societies had lived alongside each other; now they had to deal with each other on a daily basis. Those who moved from West to East in the first few months grew used to being ignored at the corner shop or served with marked unfriendliness. Easterners wanted to forget all about the Wall, and freedom of movement was one of their main demands. They'd never imagined that when the Wall was gone people would come to them – and not just to visit.

Half of the flats in Dietrich's house were unoccupied. He lived there for fifteen years before moving just around the corner. In that time, he founded an agency and for years he ran online campaigns for the SPD, the Social Democratic Party. He still has a hint of his original North German accent. In GDR times, the area north of Wilhelm-Pieck-Strasse (later renamed Torstrasse) wasn't an attractive place to live. Here, there were none of the East German bohemians of Prenzlauer Berg. Young families and people with ambitions were moving to the newly built estates on the edge of the city offering new apartments equipped with running hot water and central heating. The old buildings in Mitte, on the other hand, had traditional tiled stoves or small gas heaters, and many ground-floor flats were blighted by mould.

'No one had a car. There were only four or five Trabants parked in the whole of Schröderstrasse when I moved in. There wasn't a single tree, and it was drab, drab, drab', Dietrich says.

It had always been a poor neighbourhood. In the mid-eighteenth century, King Frederick the Great instructed his officials to study whether the carpenters and masons from Saxony and the Vogtland employed on Berlin's royal building projects during the summer could not be settled outside the city's northern gates. First, the workers wouldn't spend their money elsewhere in the winter, and second, the Prussian state sorely needed to boost its population. The king enticed the workers to stay by allowing them to earn a good winter crust from spinning, and they were also exempt from excise tax because their homes were in Linienstrasse and thus outside the Customs Wall. As Julius Rodenberg noted at the end of the nineteenth century, Neu-Vogtland soon degenerated into a 'notorious place of poverty and misery where no one ventures of his own accord'. Rodenberg had seen the small colonist houses of the original Neu-Vogtland with his own eyes.

A pamphlet published in 1788 characterized Neu-Vogtland as a 'suburb outside Rosenthaler Tor which has always been a bolthole for large thieving mobs. Since it lies in open countryside beyond the curtain wall, the wanton rabble must never fear attack and can go about their wicked business in the surrounding villages and along the high road.' Forty years later, a text about Berlin described Neu-Vogtland as 'the headquarters of the mob'. The carpenters had been succeeded by a proletariat of weavers, wool spinners and hired labourers for whom the suburb provided a cheap place to live. The colonist houses and the later family houses, where hundreds of poor people lived cheek by jowl, were demolished and replaced after 1872 by new tenement buildings when Berlin expanded beyond the old city limits.

Over a hundred years later, the atmosphere around Schröderstrasse was still overwhelmingly proletarian. Entering the block bordered by Invalidenstrasse, Chausseestrasse, Wilhelm Picck-Strasse and Gartenstrasse was like setting foot in a clearly delineated territory. Intruders were immediately clocked, sized up and, in some circumstances, subjected to a few choice remarks.

However, Dietrich Boelter was quickly accepted in his new neighbourhood because he got on well with Marco, who was respected by the whole street. 'Know him and you had nothing to fear.'

Over generations, the residents of the old suburb had grown mistrustful of anyone in a position of authority while also developing their own particular brand of self-confidence. Dietrich still sensed this old Berliner proletarian mentality on his block.

'The pint-and-chaser drinkers were still around then. Some had been forcibly assigned a job. They were totally down on socialism, but that didn't make them reactionary. They watched Western television, were well informed and had often taken to drink. These were the people the state had tried to keep quiet by putting a bit of pressure on them to work.'

The local youngsters were street-smart city-dwellers and quickly adapted to the new situation.

'When I moved into the street, a few lads there were surfing the techno wave. They all had short-cropped peroxide-blond hair. One of them lived in our building. He always wore white jeans, and there was always a party in his flat and a constant stream of people going in and out. I suspect he was pushing ecstasy. Then one day he moved out, just like that', Dietrich says.

The corner bar was a haunt of pimps and prostitutes but also attracted a nebulous right-wing crowd.

'Inside, the attitude was, "We don't want any gays coming in here. We won't beat them up, but we will chuck them out"', Boelter says.

Given that there was a gay bar just around the corner, that was probably nothing but tough talk.

Eva Otaño Ugarte was living in the same neighbourhood shortly after the fall of the Wall. She and a girlfriend had come from Spain to Berlin in September 1989. Now she lives in Kreuzberg, where she works as a graphic designer.

'We wanted to have a holiday, travel on to Prague, see the Eastern Bloc.' But she liked it in West Berlin. 'Then the

Wall came down and I decided to stay for a year. I immediately headed east.'

She lived at Tacheles for a week, but it was draughty; there was barely a single intact window. She found a flat in Bergstrasse and, like so many others who had only planned to visit East Berlin for a little while after the Wende, she got stuck in Mitte.

'You've got a cheap place to live, you can experiment . . . and party of course. I'm glad I experienced it. I feel very privileged.'

Eva lived in squats. She hardly spoke any German, but she needed work. Hearing that a club was opening up in the cellar of Tacheles, she went to Ständige Vertretung on its very first night. Then when they were looking for someone to run the till, she got the gig. Eva started taking photographs, but although she had enough money to live on, she didn't always have enough to buy and develop films. She had three cameras stolen, one of which she later found in a second hand shop in Friedrichstrasse. 'The same place I'd bought it in 1990.' It wasn't just her financial circumstances that made photography hard, though. 'The atmosphere wasn't right for photographing everyday life. It was all about living, living, living! People tended to do more artistic photography. Other things were more important to the Germans. They wanted change, and fast.'

She ate her first currywurst at a sausage stand in a vacant plot on the corner of Invalidenstrasse and Ackerstrasse. The former building had been destroyed by a bomb. The snack stand on Ackerstrasse was the only one far and wide and open 'day and night'. In Eva's photo of the fast-food joint, taken one characteristically wintry Berlin day, the corner looks pretty grim. An elderly couple walk past in long coats. The stand's new sign sports the logo of a traditional West Berlin brewery called Schultheiss.

'There were so many things to discover. East German culture, for example', Eva says. 'We had no idea about any of it,
the politics, the whole system. One system had fallen apart,
communism, and now a new system was on its way in. The
same thing happened in Spain. There was the transition from
dictatorship to democracy when Franco died. For ten years,
everything was exciting. It was as if the country had been
born again. What I also noticed in East Berlin, though, was
that over time it seemed more and more like colonization.'

The first free and democratic elections for the East Berlin
city assembly are held on 6 May 1990. The majority of East
Berliners vote for left-wing candidates: the SPD comes first
with a good third of the votes, followed by the PDS [Party
of Democratic Socialism, the successor party to the SED]
with 30 per cent. The SPD and the CDU [the Christian
Democratic Union] form a 'grand coalition' and elect Tino
Schwierzina mayor of East Berlin.

Thomas Krüger, the Kirche von Unten vicar and a founding member of the Social Democratic Party in East Germany,
is elected a city councillor and takes charge of the office of
internal affairs. Thorsten Schilling is appointed press secretary. For someone who studied Marxism-Leninism and was
ordered to leave the country within four hours on account of
subversive activities, it is a curious career move, but at a time
of so many surprises, it is passed over without comment.

Only a few months back, they and other dissidents and
opposition leaders were contesting the power of a party that
targeted adversaries of the status quo via countless 'operative procedures' enacted by hundreds of thousands of Stasi
informers. Opposition figures elected to political office
come up against the very administrative apparatus they
have until recently been fighting. Krüger's predecessor is
the man whose signature stripped Thorsten Schilling of his

nationality. The boss is no longer there, but the secretary and the driver are still in post.

'I found it a strange case of historical hermeneutics coming full circle. Krüger's driver was a really nice guy, but people like him might have been the ones taking you to jail before', Thorsten says.

In his file he discovers that his contacts with Western journalists had led to accusations of espionage – a charge that could have meant a long prison sentence. Now the chauffeur comes to fetch him every day at six, picking up Thorsten and his colleagues on a loop and then driving them out to Hohenschönhausen.

The council office for internal affairs is in the grounds of the Ministry for State Security's Main Directorate for Reconnaissance. East German civil servants start work at seven in the morning, and the day begins with initial briefings.

'Seasoned Western officials tried to give some structure to a somewhat cumbersome Eastern political machinery that had a lot to learn', Schilling says. The East Berliners have already been at work for two hours by the time the staff members and consultants from West Berlin roll in at nine. 'There was this classic situation when someone would ask, "Have you read this?" and their colleague would say, "How could I have read it? I only just got here."'

The reunification of the two halves of the city is more than just a clash of systems and mentalities, but at least the clocks are synchronized. When the Red Army occupied Berlin in May 1945, the city's clocks were adjusted to Moscow time so that the administrative working days were aligned.

Many 'contaminated' middle managers in the civil service are sacked after the Wende, and everyone else prepares for transfer to agencies of the new Senate following the first Berlin-wide elections. But what is to be done with all the local government officials, especially senior civil servants, responsible for implementing SED policy?

Councillor Krüger drafts the so-called 'New Broom Resolution', no. 27/90. The idea suggested to him by his Western colleagues seems both simple and fair: the relevant individuals are to leave their posts, quit the civil service and then reapply. Anyone with no black marks against their name who is rehired is henceforth above suspicion and paid the same salary as Western staff. The proposal provokes outrage.

'Politically, it was totally naïve', Thorsten says. 'The same demand was valid for everyone, whether they'd done something wrong or not. It was applied, for instance, to Berlin Zoo director and national hero Professor Heinrich Dathe, to the director and actors of the Maxim Gorki Theater, the Deutsches Theater and so on. Overnight, we had everyone against us.'

Two days later, protesters occupy the Rotes Rathaus, East Berlin's red-brick city hall. Hundreds of angry citizens demand the withdrawal of the measures. When the furious crowd storms the building, Thorsten suddenly finds himself face to face with two of his friends.

'To them I had become the enemy. I was a traitor. Everyone active in dissident circles viewed politics as treachery. It was an inexcusable act. It wasn't cool. All of a sudden, you found yourself in the opposite camp. My mates and I often used to go to the Eimer, the punk squat and pub in Rosenthaler Strasse. It wasn't long before they kicked us out. Speiche, the superpunk of East Berlin, recognized us and yelled, "We don't want any politicians like you here. Get out!"'

Not long afterwards, Speiche was outed as having worked for the Stasi. Whole milieus and long-standing friendships were torn asunder. People from the West often found it hard to see the rifts in East German society. They could feel a kind of interference in the air, but their antennae weren't sensitive enough to decode a form of communication honed over decades and based on inserting and reading messages between the lines. Few Westerners knew that the Stasi's corrosive efforts had often focused on families and groups of mates and between friends. It's difficult to imagine what it's like to be spied on by your friends, your children, your wife or husband.

Meanwhile, inside the occupied city hall there are frantic discussions about what to do.

'So Mayor Tino Schwierzina steps forward and says, "I apologize, folks. That was a mistake, and I take it back. Your demands will be met, but please go home now." But they didn't go home. Then he said three times, "You can trust me!" An hour later the city hall was empty again and closed off. No one else was allowed in. Then there was a meeting. That's when the administrative lawyers came into play, analysing what the politicians said and how their words might be interpreted. The conclusion was that the resolution should be redrafted. The relevant people would be checked and even though it was never implemented to the letter, the main concerns were addressed. No one had to resign, and the will of the people was partially accommodated.'

Not that it made much difference. Ten thousand demonstrators gathered on the square outside the city hall on Thomas Krüger's birthday, clamouring for him to resign. The people had wrested control of the streets from the SED and now they refused to go home. From one day to the next, the opposition figures who had themselves been organizing demos until very recently had to learn to govern an East Berlin that had developed an appetite for protest. Each new political conflict brought hordes of people out into the streets.

'A few thousand people would march through the streets to the Rathaus, and every time, somehow, everything was at stake. It was a similar atmosphere to the recent protests against Stuttgart 21.[6] The streets as a site of direct democracy enacted by angry citizens', Thorsten says.

Sometimes, though, those angry citizens faced him across his desk.

'Some of the old SED cadres couldn't cover their living costs, now they were retired, from their pension. They would stand there, staring you in the eye, and you knew they might go for your throat at any moment.'

In 1990 it wasn't only on the dance floor and in bars that you needed to be physically present to be part of the story.

'It was a very physical period in politics. Later, as councillor for internal affairs, Krüger was assigned bodyguards because the situation started to get dangerous', Thorsten Schilling says. Before it got to that point, however, the public would demonstrate, debate and express its mistrust of all forms of politics.

By day Thorsten helped to organize the transition to a working democracy; in the evenings he toured Mitte's bars and clubs. One place he frequented was the Gogo Bar in a squat on Neue Schönhauser Strasse where they played seventies music like Sweet and T. Rex. A large glass of whisky cost five marks.

'The squats didn't charge much and they also served big shots. I did that a few times – spent the whole night standing by the bar, chatting to people. I would sometimes go clubbing

---

[6] The reference here is to the wave of petitions and protests triggered by a construction project (begun in 2010) to upgrade Stuttgart's main-line railway and underground links and the city's central station. Opposition to the project is partially credited with sweeping the Greens to control of Stuttgart city council.

at the Tresor and on to the office early the next morning, for my press secretary job, all done up in suit and tie. It was good to go to the occupied places in the evenings because you could see that East Berlin was in a transitional phase. It wouldn't stay that way, though. The directives approved during the day were designed to apply West Berlin's laws.'

Until the reunification of the city and of the country, Berlin was governed by a dual structure in the West and the East, known colloquially as MagiSenat [a portmanteau of 'Magistrat' (East) and 'Senat' (West)]. East Berlin's Magistrat or council was tasked with ensuring that public bodies complied with Western norms and standards.

The transition from one system to another was taking its time, though, and this could be felt everywhere.

'No one was in control of the streets', Ben de Biel recalls. 'One time, we sneaked into the children's swimming pool in Monbijou park. We set candles afloat and swam around. Then the police turned up and said it wasn't allowed. And we went, "Yeah, but we're not causing any trouble." So they said, "All right then, but make sure you clean up afterwards." We promised we would, and we did, and then they let us carry on swimming.'

For several more years, people running unlicensed bars and clubs could rely on the fact that the police still hadn't fully assimilated the new rules.

The end of the VEBs

Turning left out of his house down Linienstrasse, five minutes was all it took Ben de Biel to get to Tacheles, where he was in charge of ensuring that the Ständige Vertretung's bar ran smoothly. Turn right and in five minutes he was at the Eimer. He later opened his own club – the Maria am

Ostbahnhof. Like many other clubs, the Maria had to move on after a while, and even at its new site it was under constant threat of closure. Ben joined the Berlin Pirate Party and as its press secretary he criticized the Senate's lack of support for the city's club culture.

He doesn't miss those early years in Mitte. 'It was a unique historical event. Everyone who was lucky enough to live here at the time can count themselves fortunate – that sort of thing comes around only once in your life. That much was clear to me when I arrived in Berlin in 1990. But it was also a historical anachronism – a half-empty city you could appropriate. There may well have been times when a city was left half empty due to war, but then people took away everything that mattered to them. Here, though, they left everything behind. We would stand out in the street and watch. No light in the windows of the first floor of Linienstrasse 144 for three days meant there was no one living there any more. So we opened the door and took a look around. There was a coffee cup still standing on the kitchen table. The owner had run off to the West, little anticipating that the West would come to him.' The monetary union and the accompanying economic and social union between the Federal Republic of Germany and the GDR came into force on 1 July 1990.

The Eimer squatters in Rosenthaler Strasse protested at the imminent arrival of capitalist conditions through the Sterntaler campaign, which Ulrike Steglich and Peter Kratz describe in their book *Das falsche Scheunenviertel* [*The Other Scheunenviertel*]:

'We want to be Westerners' was the slogan printed on the leaflets promising the blessings of Western currency for the afternoon of 15 April 1990 to the not yet currency-united Rosenthaler Strasse. 'We want to be Westerners', people were supposed to shout and then Deutschmarks would rain down on them. A different motive for the curious to come to Rosenthaler Strasse that afternoon was their disbelief that anyone would subject themselves to such humiliation. However, enough people came that the police were forced to block the tram route. Just as their necks were beginning to ache, onlookers – some obediently chanting the suggested slogan, the more cunning among them turning their umbrellas upside down – finally got what they'd been waiting for. A handful of pennies came raining down from the roof of a house on the other side of the road.

Many small companies didn't survive long in the teeth of Western competition.

'It all happened at unimaginable speed after monetary union. Every day another shop would close down and put its contents out on the pavement, and every day we received a new delivery', Ben de Biel says.

The residents of Kleine Hamburger Strasse were given a container full of pelts by the last furrier in Mitte. They used them to line their winter clothes and still had enough left over to wrap up the street lamp outside their house in fur.

'A week later there was this cardboard box, three metres by six, full of hats and other headgear from the GDR children's circus. So now we had about 600 different items of headgear, mostly for small heads, but still. And a few of the performers were obviously adults. In performances of *Jim Knopf*, for example. The next day someone turned up with five large buckets of this amazing blue paint, totally toxic. We painted the whole house with the stuff', Ben de Biel says.

Although abandoned flats were generally locked and it required a ritual act of violence to break down the door, some factory compounds and administrative buildings were wide open. You could just walk in. Often the phones still worked, and people would make long-distance calls to friends and family in Bavaria, England or Spain. The employees had left their desks all neat and tidy when they closed the doors behind themselves for the final time. Some desks still had documents and sharpened pencils lying on them, as if their occupants had merely popped out for lunch. The cafeterias were no longer in use either.

'We could help ourselves to the Mitropa crockery in the cupboards because it had all been abandoned anyway', Christoph Keller remembers. Around the corner from his flat were Sekura's extensive premises in Chausseestrasse, but the only part still in business was a small shop where you could buy office supplies for a song, as well as the portraits of Honecker that once hung in entrances and above desks. 'A company with 5,000 employees had closed down overnight', Christoph adds.

The flip sides of these eerily empty factories and official buildings, the free telephones and suddenly unwanted fittings, were unemployment and uncertainty. All these sites had until recently been workplaces, but now many companies were 'wound up'. The Treuhandanstalt or 'trust agency' was handed the task of privatizing and restoring the East German VEBs [Volkseigene Betriebe; publicly owned enterprises] to profitability. The Treuhand's headquarters were in Goering's former Ministry of Aviation. It closed unprofitable factories and sold off state property – an opportunity for certain entrepreneurs to do some very tidy business. The side effects of this historically unprecedented privatization drive were misuse of public funds and white-collar crime. By the end of 1994 the agency managed to privatize slightly over half of the VEBs, and just under a third were shut down. Some reverted to their former owners, but very few were transferred into collective ownership. A total of two and a half million industrial jobs were slashed in East Germany because so many uncompetitive companies foundered in the free market.

'It wasn't only their jobs that people lost; it was their entire value system. Alcohol was one answer, and so was violence', Christoph Keller recalls. A woman living next door to him had just graduated with a first-class economics degree in the Soviet Union and was retraining to become an artist. 'She had psychological problems because she was unable to cope with the upheaval, either financially or economically. That kind of thing was a daily occurrence. There was a flasher living with his sister in my building and also a man prone to violence. Lots of buildings saw similar things, like grandmas living in their pets' faeces.'

Having lived for years on the margins of the capital of the GDR, the residents of Mitte had been catapulted into a new world and not all of them could deal with it.

Eva Otaño Ugarte observed the same uncertainty among her friends. 'The first four or five years were one big party, and people got through them. It was only later that frustration began to set in. My Eastern friends had lots of illusions and lots of energy, but they also had lots of problems and a huge fear of the unknown.'

Most East Germans were initially euphoric, but then they started to travel and form their own opinions.

'A friend of mine went to Majorca for six months', Eva says. 'She learned Spanish and worked there. Majorca is a prime example of unfettered tourism, capitalism in its purest form. Having never encountered anything like it before, she was shocked.'

The dramatic changes affected everyone's lives, yet they were most manifest in the fate of objects that had been left lying around in the deserted factories, in abandoned apartments, in the middle of the street, but were then put to new purposes.

The inhabitants of Mitte had access to an abundance of materials that seemed to have become useless overnight and that no one deemed worth keeping. The streets were littered with things that had been thrown out 'merely because they had "GDR" on them', Ben de Biel says. They represented a past that everyone wanted to leave behind and no one wanted in their living room.

'Begrüssungsgeld' ['welcome money'] distributed by the West German government, combined with monetary reforms, triggered a first wave of binge-buying in the East. Suddenly, a whole world of colourful Western goods was within reach. Native East Berliners got rid of their furniture and went shopping at IKEA in Spandau. Ironically, many of the products on offer at the Swedish furniture store with the friendly image had once been made in East German factories, where the GDR assigned some political prisoners to furniture production. In many streets, heaps of discarded interior furnishings reached some metres high, and newcomers sifted through them in search of salvageable items.

Fig. 7 Looking for discards in Linienstrasse, 1990

Ben de Biel photographed his flatmate Dagmar going about her favourite activity – inspecting what other people have thrown away. In her bucket-top boots and miniskirt, Dagmar is on her tiptoes, her head and arms already deep inside the rubbish skip she is scouring. The living room of their house in Kleine Hamburger Strasse was a hotchpotch of capitalist-produced and socialist-made objects and symbols. The living room table was a surfboard, striking a pleasing contrast with a Honecker portrait hanging on one wall.

It wasn't only in living rooms and squats that the owner-less things from the vanished state embarked on a second life. Many items escaped oblivion by being put to fresh use as material for installations and the interiors of bars, clubs and lounges. One particularly famous fixture was the bar that Fred Rubin carefully dismantled in the Palast der Republik, the former East German parliament. Segments of it were repurposed in one of the later WMF clubs.

'They were unique pieces. The bar in the Palast der Republik, aka Erich's Lamp Shop, wasn't old, you know. The Palace had only been completed ten years earlier', Ben says. 'The state could have rented a warehouse – there was enough space. If someone had been smart, they would've stored all those things because they were, after all, histori-cally significant.'

Objects that had until recently been part of everyday life were examined with archaeological interest and assessed in terms of their historical and aesthetic value. Generally, they were treated with respect.

'To say there was a code of honour would be inaccurate, but we would complain if someone deliberately broke some-thing', Christoph Keller says. 'Even if it was obvious that no one was going to claim the items and that the buildings were potentially going to be torn down, people took it badly if someone vandalized things. I didn't like it when people got cocky and started smashing windows. Those places were all monuments – monuments to a particular history, monuments to the present moment.'

The artists Bastiaan Maris, Gordon Monahan and Laura Kikauka ran the Glowing Pickle out of a garage in Brunnenstrasse, and everyone heading for the Boudoir had to walk past it. The Boudoir was a salon on one of the upper floors off a back courtyard, and in its centre stood a bed. In the Glowing Pickle, the outhouse downstairs, the artists collected technical devices that state enterprises, the Humboldt Universität or the Charité hospital had discarded or dumped in skips. Eastern Bloc technical equipment was stacked up to the ceiling on shelves: ion beamers, a Czech analogue computer, high-voltage generators, voltmeters from Poland, mass spectrometers, electronic calculators, plotters and, last but not least, two document shredders and a massage machine. The Glowing Pickle was a museum that preserved the memory of a lost civilization but resembled a Third World electronics store.

However, the most spectacular artefacts on display in Mitte were two old fighter planes from the Soviet Union.

'We were driving through Brandenburg and suddenly there were these signs saying "Restricted military area. You will be shot"', Ben de Biel recalls. 'But we'd already heard that it was totally abandoned. We drove through a wood and after a while we came to a clearing where we saw two MiGs. There were two railway wagons standing on thirty metres of track. The tracks were disconnected, and the MiGs had been gutted. It was a place where the Soviets had practised disassembling the wings and loading them on to pontoon boats. The guys from the Mutoid Waste Company bought them from the Russians.'

The Mutoid Waste Company was founded in London. Its members built machines based on the *Mad Max* movies' post-apocalyptic aesthetic and organized acid house parties in disused factories. Following a series of police raids on their London industrial site in 1989, the Mutoids moved to West Berlin. After the fall of the Wall, they started collecting abandoned military equipment. They paid a total of 400 Deutschmarks for those two MiGs. However, the planes weren't actually the property of the former Soviet army: the training area in Strausberg used to belong to the East German Nationale Volksarmee, which had since been absorbed by the West German Bundeswehr. Although the army didn't notice the material's absence, a vigilant pensioner tipped them off about the theft.

Officers from the criminal investigations agency later traced the planes to a spot near the Reichstag. The artists of the Mutoid Waste Company had installed the interceptor plane to make it look as if it had crashed into a former East German border watchtower. The installation was supposed to symbolize an incident in a war that was never fought. Though not particularly impressive politically or artistically, its bizarreness proved a hit with both locals and tourists. Even the police showed some sympathy for the artists and left them to get on with it. The commander of the 5th Division of the German Air Force ultimately allowed the Mutoid Waste Company to keep the remains of the two jets.

Military junk was a perfect match for the aesthetic style cultivated by many squats and bars. Squatters and bar managers tended to leave places just as they found them to allow the charm of what had been left behind to work its magic and create a sense of timelessness. Unplastered walls gradually became a distinctive feature of the new Berlin style, signalling an intention to take up residence for a limited and undefined period of time. There was no point in spending hours of energy repairing and painting walls you had just scraped free of layers of wallpaper decades old and several centimetres thick – you'd be moving on in a year or two anyway. Instead, you could decorate the empty rooms with whatever you found in the street.

The squats of Mitte took the cyberpunk style that had emerged in West Berlin in the late eighties to even greater heights. The Dead Chickens in Haus Schwarzenberg at Hackescher Markt built comical monsters out of junk metal and fitted them with sophisticated hydraulics to make them move. They are still a tourist attraction today.

The furniture in Café Zapata at Tacheles and Café Silberstein on Oranienburger Strasse was welded together, its rusty surface suggesting that it was older than it really was. The prevailing style of the interior decorations and furniture in Mitte was a kind of futuristic revamp of Biedermeier or rococo. Scrap metal, bulky waste and discarded devices were used to create new, extravagantly embellished interior designs. At first sight they seemed to represent an aesthetic counter-manifesto to the 'Gelsenkirchen baroque' of German lower-middle-class flats and yet, on closer inspection, they revealed a similar fondness for adornment. The squat clubs also had a kind of shabby cosiness. Maybe it was intended as a parody of comfort, but it may also have stemmed from a longing for comfort where a certain amount of dirt is accepted. Whichever way, the style of the squatters and their pubs was neither elegant nor glamorous, and there was absolutely nothing rigid or strict about it. Of all the first-generation squatter clubs and bars, the sole exception to this sensibility was Ständige Vertretung, with its mobile bar on springs and its clean, clinical laser beam bisecting the room in a departure from the nostalgia of the post-war period.

One of Ben de Biel's photos shows squatters having breakfast in Kleine Hamburger Strasse. (A freshly washed shirt on a coat hanger in figure 5, a photo he took later at the same address, suggests that people weren't only partying

Fig. 8 Breakfast at Kleine Hamburger Strasse 5 in 1990

and collecting material but clearly going out to work too.) A child is sitting up at the table on its father's or mother's lap. Children were born and raised, just not necessarily in a nuclear family; in the early days they were more commonly part of a squatter clan. The general impression is somewhat chaotic but nonetheless homely.

The squatters were the avant-garde of the new middle-class movement drawn to all the space in the old Spandauer and Rosenthaler Vorstadt after the fall of the Wall. Kleine Hamburger Strasse is now in a nice residential area. Even Schröderstrasse, which retained its character for a long time and was once one of the darkest and most run-down streets in Mitte, has now been spruced up. For two hundred and fifty years it was home to the poor and the underprivileged, but the neighbourhood's metamorphosis into a popular middle-class district took only another twenty.

Where there was once a corner pub is now the office of the Alpenblick bakery, right next door, whose owners also run the Alpenblick restaurant on the opposite corner. A Food Factory, various sophisticated interior decorators and the Studio Schöne Mitte for 'regenerative cosmetics and body-sculpting' furnish all the ingredients of the new middle-class lifestyle. The residents of old haven't all moved out. The old corner pub's regulars have found a new, admittedly much smaller place a few buildings away. Kollwitzplatz has become an expensive area as well as the epitome of social homogeneity. There are very few old and poor people, and the migrants who live here generally come from Western Europe.

From squatting to temporary licence

In the best-case scenario, anarchy is a social framework that tries to get by without hierarchies, exploitation and violence.

After the fall of the Wall, it was not anarchy that ruled in Mitte, even though the state of the authorities sometimes came very close to the anarchist ideal. Wherever the spirit of revolution was present, civil servants strove to discharge their duties in the least authoritarian way possible and in open dialogue with the public. During the transition from one system to another, the authorities here were more inclined to experiment than they were elsewhere to see if it was possible to come up with a less hierarchical model of community living. East German citizens had experienced the peaceful revolution of 1989, while young Westerners had been shaped by a more permissive post-1968 society. These two groups met and mingled in bars and squats, and at basement parties.

Mainzer Strasse emerged as the centre of the new squatter movement. There was a house for queens, a women's and lesbian house, a 'Sponti' house,[7] a party house, a hippie house and an anti-imperialist house. The queens' house contained the only gay pub in the whole of Friedrichshain. Probably the only thing the inhabitants of Mainzer Strasse had in common was that they all preferred to hang out in their own autonomous spaces. Anarchy involves a willingness to deal with a wide variety of lifestyles and allowing people to express their wishes spontaneously; anarchists require no declaration of intentions and objectives.

> The movement exploded all categories to facilitate in time and space happenings involving unique, unrepeatable possibilities. It reduced the world to a stage on which you yourself could be an actor and no longer merely a spectator of mass-media events. The movement was a temporal phenomenon – the irruption of a different time into normal time, the extraction from the everyday of a time space with its own rules,

a certain R.Adi.Ator writes in the foreword to the German edition of the Dutch agency Adilkno's book about the squatters who built a new movement in Amsterdam, Berlin, London, Paris, Zurich and other cities from the 1970s onwards. The English translation, *Cracking the Movement*, was published in New York in 1994.

In autumn 1990, when the red–green-dominated Senate orders the clearing of the Mainzer Strasse squats in Friedrichshain, it sends a clear signal that all this living in

---

[7] The so-called 'Spontis' were a left-wing avant-garde movement that developed in various German cities in the 1970s and 1980s. They believed in the need for spontaneous happenings, including street theatre, as a tool of revolutionary change.

the moment and transitional anarchy cannot go on for ever. A clash between police and squatters is triggered by the evictions of the occupants of two buildings in nearby Pfarrstrasse. The Mainzer squatters fear that they too will have to abandon their houses and so on 12 November they erect barricades several metres high, gouge trenches in the road with a stolen digger and hurl stones at the police. The police drive an armoured engineering vehicle along the street and fire tear gas through open windows. The squatters respond by throwing flares. They summarily declare their neighbourhood a 'liberated zone', and expel all photographers and camera operators because they regard 'the media' as the greatest enemy of immediate experience.

Hard-line anarchists, many of them from Kreuzberg, try to defend their territory and orchestrate a new chapter in their struggle against the system. 'We have to conclude that for some people it was no longer simply about legalizing their housing and living arrangements but about creating unregulated autonomous areas inspired by the legendary example of West Berlin squats, i.e. lawless zones. Many buildings were squatted to destruction', recalls Bernd Finger, who was head of the Magistrat's department of public order and security at the time.

Twenty-year-old lads, otherwise only interested in sex, music and parties like every other kid their age, travel to Friedrichshain to help build barricades and throw stones. Hooligans from Lichtenberg lend the squatters a hand. They may simply be taking advantage of the exceptional situation in a form of existentialist extreme sport, but a lot of other people appear to be rebelling against a clampdown on urban space, the beginning of political solutions and the return of an everyday routine no one is pining for. The sound of the Wende in those few days consists of sirens, helicopters and stones colliding with cobbles.

The sound of the police sirens has already changed. Those who moved from West to East in early 1990 are surprised by the tone of approaching Volkspolizei patrol cars. Rather than a tinny 'dee-da', the sirens here resemble those they've heard in American gangster films. At night, through open windows, East Berlin sounds like New York.

Over the summer, the East Berlin Magistrat adopts the 'Berlin line of reason' – the term the West Berlin Senate, led by city mayor Hans-Jochen Vogel, coined for its policy of evicting squatters within twenty-four hours in 1981. Existing squats are specifically exempt from this rule and only to be cleared if the owner applies formally for penal action and promises to start renovating the building within a reasonable period of time. The battle over such houses degenerated into increasingly violent clashes in the early eighties, and eventually a demonstrator died. Intellectuals and church leaders declared themselves guardians of individual buildings. Many citizens would no longer countenance a purely law-and-order solution to the squats or a crackdown on the movement.

The Magistrat toes the Berlin line on 24 July 1990, when there are about 130 squats in East Berlin.

'As in West Berlin, they set a cut-off date and after that the people could own the buildings. It worked too. We frequently went into squats. We calmed things down in a very reformist spirit. Mainzer Strasse, on the other hand, was a whole complex, with lots of houses in a small area. It was more complicated, both from an urban management point of view and from a cultural perspective', Thorsten Schilling recalls.

Although the first buildings have been squatted months before the deadline, Senate, Magistrat and East Berlin's assembly all believe that the previous incidents leave them no choice but to clear the street.

'The SPD, the West Berlin SPD of all people, were desperate to "make a stand" on this, as the saying goes. They were obviously running scared of the CDU's argument that left-wingers were incapable of enforcing the law', Thorsten Schilling says.

City mayor Tino Schwierzina and his minister for internal affairs, Thomas Krüger, try until the very last to negotiate in the spirit of 1989. They hold meetings with delegations from the various squats.

'These youngsters – think lawyers' sons – would turn up at the Rotes Rathaus to see Schwierzina and put on their West German act, you know: "We're in the right and here are our demands!" There was no constructive communication whatsoever. We were faced with these robots churning out statements, pumped up with indignation and spouting the most extreme demands', Thorsten remembers. 'At the next meeting we'd have all these outraged East Berliners, shouting, "Kick them out of there, or I'm going to buy myself a Kalashnikov!" It was a clash between two aggressive, excitable blocs. East Berlin's well-drilled citizens had enough on their plate just trying to survive; they had to figure out what was going to become of them. On the other hand, there were also splits in the Spassguerilla – the guerrilla revellers. We could tell the groups were culturally very distinct, and they were very much at odds over their objectives.'

Negotiations continue at a district level, but the SPD-led Senate has already decided to clear Mainzer Strasse. One day the relevant housing association and the SPD senator responsible for internal affairs insist that the Mainzer Strasse squatters can stay, but within twenty-four hours an application has been filed for their eviction.

With police units from all over Germany deployed to Berlin the day before, the scenes on the morning of 14 November are akin to civil war. Anarchists lob Molotov cocktails and stones from the roofs. Some houses have been barricaded with steel doors against raiding police officers.

Helicopters circle overhead, and the police use stun grenades. After hours of fighting, during which many residents flee in shock, police officers abseil onto the rooftops, only to find that the vast majority of the squatters have already run away.

Terrified of lasting damage to the city's image, the governing mayor of Berlin, Walter Momper, warns people not to infer from these violent clashes that Berlin was unfit to be the capital.

The clearing of Mainzer Strasse was a highly symbolic act. A few weeks after German reunification, here was the state proclaiming that the period of transition, the intermediate era, was over. Some squats sent delegates to the round tables, others didn't. Long after the Mainzer Strasse clearance, squatters continued to debate whether the right path was to consider a house an autonomous zone, opt for a formal tenancy agreement or perhaps even buy it. The direction of travel, however, was very clearly towards ownership.

Decrying the SPD's actions, the Alternative Liste brought down the first red–green coalition, which had governed Berlin since 1989. The leader of the Alternative Liste's parliamentary group, Renate Künast, declared the red–green experiment a failure and accused the SPD of provoking a wave of violence. There was no need to clear Mainzer Strasse: 'There are 27,000 empty flats in East Berlin.'

Walter Momper replied that 45,000 people were looking for somewhere to live in the eastern part of Berlin, and most of the existing stock was uninhabitable. 'It is unacceptable for some people to try to jump the housing queue, which is especially long in East Berlin, and seize any living space they can use.'

The CDU won the elections on 2 December 1990. Eberhard Diepgen, who had risen through the party ranks in West Berlin, formed a grand coalition with the SPD and was re-elected governing mayor, but this time of the whole city. To the disgust of many of his SPD comrades, Momper abandoned politics for a job in real estate.

The West Berlin establishment had taken control. After the clearances, a district mayor of Prenzlauer Berg was quoted in the press as saying that the SPD's eviction of the squatters had been an attempt to seize the moral high ground on the eve of the elections: 'They aren't interested in us. Basically, we're an occupied country.'

East German civil rights activists from the Neues Forum were enraged by the ferocity of street fighters from the West and by the brutality of the police. They didn't want to have to watch 'Western police officers and hard-line Western anarchists slugging it out over here'. For many East Berliners who had recently protested against the SED, it came as a shock to see water cannon turned against their fellow citizens.

'Helios Mendiburu, the then mayor of Friedrichshain, stood in front of the water cannon,' Thorsten Schilling says, 'but he had no chance of stopping it.'

The clearance of Mainzer Strasse offered further proof to many East Berliners that their experiences and political opinions counted for nothing.

'The "unification agreement" is not an agreement about unification, but a unilateral agreement. In structure it follows the logic of successor states', the legal scholar Ulrich K. Preuss writes in September 1990 regarding the imminent reunification. On 3 October 1990 a country that had continued to exist only on paper was dissolved and folded into a different state.

The first free East German Volkskammer elections in March 1990 disappointed all those hoping for a 'Third Way' of gentle, reformed socialism. With the opening of the Wall, it was no longer a viable option for the GDR to go it alone; the introduction of free movement made experimenting impossible.

Dietrich Boelter was actively involved in a music and cartoon magazine called *Wart's Up!* at the time, a post-Wende project that brought Westerners and Easterners together, although East Germans were in the majority. Here too, the sense of a fresh start didn't last long.

'Pessimism overcame what was still the GDR when the Allianz für Deutschland – a conservative electoral coalition put together by Helmut Kohl and including the East German CDU, the Deutsche Soziale Union and Demokratischer Aufbruch [Democratic Awakening] – won an overall majority. We were sitting together in Prenzlauer Allee and agreed that nothing would come of the Third Way now, nothing new stood any chance. That was a crushing feeling', Dietrich Boelter says.

He saw the verve of the early days subside, and the initiators of *Wart's Up!*, who had until then been collaborating closely on their project, began to harp on about their Western or Eastern origins again. Even before reunification was celebrated on 3 October 1990, the country split into two camps, 'Ossis' and 'Wessis', a divide that was to last for many years – and this time no Wall was required.

In the absence of a Third Way, the transition still offered opportunities to sustain the spirit of the peaceful revolution, at least for the moment and on a small scale. One of the revolution's achievements was the round tables where citizens could discuss matters with officials and politicians. In the municipal elections, dissident cultural leaders and people from Neues Forum and Bündnis 90 [Alliance 90] were voted in as district councillors and took on responsibility for urban development and culture. They adopted a pragmatic approach to dealing with the uncertainty of the interregnum and making the many empty premises in the city centre available to people with cultural projects.

Jutta Weitz, who was in charge of commercial premises for the Berlin-Mitte housing association, was delighted if someone had other plans than to open a video shop, an amusement arcade, a tax consultant's office or a dental surgery. She got on well with the many crazy people looking for studios or dreaming up weird art projects and tried to find them spaces to work in. The end of the anarchic period gave way to the era of temporary licence.

Talk to anyone who was active in Mitte after the Wende and sooner or later they will mention Jutta Weitz's name, adding that she deserves a medal or the Federal Cross of Merit.[8]

'Things would look completely different here in Mitte if it weren't for Jutta Weitz. The earth would have been scorched much earlier.'

This carries a hint of adulation or the cult of personality, but it's an accurate description nonetheless. If Jutta hadn't introduced the practice of finding spaces for artists to use on licence, far less art would have come out of Mitte and the club scene would not have kept discovering new nooks to squat. The district would quite simply never have grown into the cultural centre whose reputation still defines the city . . . and yet Jutta Weitz's appointment and subsequent rise to become a leading figure of the 'temporary licence' era can be traced back to a hare-brained idea.

Jutta comes from a long-established Berlin family, something you cannot fail to notice because not only does she have a strong local accent but she is also armed with the city's characteristic wit. As a young woman, she worked first in the

---

[8]   She was indeed awarded the Berlin Order of Merit in 2020.

department for concerts and touring theatre of East Berlin council, then at the Prater in Kastanienallee, one of the East German capital's larger local cultural centres. There was something on every night, but Jutta had two children and felt like the odd evening off.

One evening a country and western band was performing at the Prater, and one of the musicians complained about his boring job at the municipal housing office. He said he'd prefer to work evenings like Jutta. They sat down after a performance to draw up a plan. People were swapping flats in East Berlin, so why shouldn't the same be possible for jobs? The two of them decided to resign and apply for each other's jobs.

'I applied for his and got it. He applied for mine and would have got it if he hadn't changed his mind and opted to remain a musician. That's what he did', Jutta explains.

She took up her new job in the labour economics department of Mitte's municipal housing office in 1988, where she was in charge of in-house cultural activities, organizing children's summer camps and brigade[9] events, and handing out medals. She had a lot of time on her hands.

'But then '89 happened, and that was the end of plodding slowly through your work.'

Her department was wound up, and the housing office restructured. The immediate priority was survey plans, and so Jutta started measuring commercial premises and flats – an experience that was to come in useful further down the line. Not long after that, a position in the commercial

---

[9] A brigade was the smallest unit within state-owned companies that was supposed to develop workers' 'socialist personality'. Membership also gave access to services such as kindergartens and clinics as well as celebrations for 1 May, Women's Day on 8 May and the anniversary of the Republic on 7 October.

department was freed up because no one wanted to work there. They were looking for someone to return buildings to their former owners – a fairly thankless task.

'No one wanted to talk to the former owners and explain why their houses were so run down. You have to stand there with old ladies and gentlemen who've got their house building back and then realize during the visit, Oh, the rain's been coming in for twenty years and no one's bothered to deal with it.'

The old buildings in Mitte were a squatter's paradise, but for many former owners and their heirs they became a complete nightmare. The ownership situation of many buildings was uncertain, partly because the GDR had declared much of the land in East Berlin and many buildings state property. On 15 June 1990 the governments of the Federal Republic and the Democratic Republic approved a joint declaration of intent to resolve open questions regarding assets. On 23 September 1990 the Volkskammer enacted the necessary legislation permitting all property expropriated after the founding of the GDR to be returned to its previous owners or their heirs. One of many exceptions to this rule related to assets seized from Jewish citizens by the Nazis. The GDR may have defined itself as an anti-fascist state, but it neither returned stolen or 'Aryanized' property nor compensated the Jewish owners. A little over a month after reunification, 24,000 pending applications for the return of property had already piled up in the various land registry offices. According to the senator overseeing the work, it took six to eight months to process each case.

Soon after the fall of the Wall, Jutta was assigned a new post within the housing department. She and a colleague were put in charge of dealing with first-time applicants to the commercial premises department and shared an office to guard against attempted bribery.

THE YEAR OF ANARCHY

'People tried just the same', Jutta says. 'Not with money, but with schnaps or sparkling wine, with flowers or by promising favours – you know, a bit of flirting. My colleague was better at dealing with people interested in going into fashion or wanting to open a tax consultancy, and I was better with the nutters and weirdos. We'd sometimes notice that an applicant was chatting to the wrong person, and so in mid-conversation we'd swap. They were happy, we were happy, and word got around.'

Soon anyone looking for a space in Mitte for their project knew that Jutta had their interests at heart. People got in touch from Australia after hearing about Jutta Weitz from friends, and her phone number was even noted on the blackboard at the PS1 contemporary art centre in New York. By this time, the municipal housing office had been renamed the Berlin-Mitte housing association (WBM).

Jutta found dealing with people a lot of fun. 'Spin it positively, and I was curious. Spin it negatively, and I was nosy', she says. 'I didn't care which field the people were working in. It was just really exciting to hear someone tell you what they were planning to do in the next few years.' As she remembers it, the priority was the need for breathing space. 'It was palpable in the city and palpable in people's heads and on a political level, at least for the short span of time when everything was up in the air. The main thing wasn't to make a quick buck but to deal with situations, social issues or new people. There was this huge curiosity – everywhere, both East and West. The central question was how do I want to live and what's possible', she remembers.

Most artists who called on Jutta wanted large spaces for the lowest possible price, but they were often satisfied with less or sharing a place with others. Some people came to see her with the most obscure projects.

'For instance, there was this one group who wanted a shop where they could lock some Berlin air inside. The place would be sealed off and opened again after three years. That was the art project: to make it possible to bottle Berlin's air.'

Nothing seemed absurd after the fall of the Wall, and Jutta was sympathetic towards every idea. Everyone wanted a space in Mitte, and Jutta was keen to satisfy the needs of everyone looking for a place to achieve their goals.

'I set out a few rules for myself. First, no one I already know will get premises by pulling strings. No societies or parties I belong to, no relations of mine. Second, my first move was to acknowledge that everyone who comes to see me has an interest and a need for space, whether I understand it or not. My principle was to try and find something for everyone. After all, they have to pay for the space. They don't get it free of charge.'

Later on, decisions about the allocation of space for art projects were taken by a round table organized by the local authority.

Jutta found it hard to turn down people making requests. It took a lot of strength and nerve, and so she decided she had to learn to say no.

'But whenever the next person came along looking for something, I thought, Oh no, say no to the next one.'

By way of compensation, she was occasionally employed as a bouncer at the Eschloraque Rümschrümpp bar in Haus Schwarzenberg, where she was allowed to let in anyone she liked. Those she didn't like had to stay outside.

'I refused to let Udo Lindenberg[10] in once, and another time it was Ben Becker.[11] I remember I said to Becker, "You

---

[10] Udo Lindenberg (b. 1946) is a German singer, drummer and composer.
[11] Ben Becker (b. 1964) is a German actor.

can send in your woman, but we don't need you right now."
It was fun. I found it easier. Ben Becker could go and drink
somewhere else; his life didn't depend on it, nor did his
career. When guys like them turned up and started yelling, I
said no. "You stupid cow", Ben Becker said.'

Celebrities had to behave themselves like everyone else in
Mitte's bars.

There would be masses of applicants standing in the hall-
way outside Jutta's office in the early days. Some had to wait
for hours until it was finally their turn. There was a lot of
pressure to go self-employed after the Wende, and Mitte was
a popular district. At some point Jutta Weitz and her colleagues stopped numbering the applications for commercial
premises because there were already well in excess of 8,000.

'There was no way you could work through them all, even
by application number. You had to see what fitted where.
And if there were fifteen applications to set up a pub in the
Oranienstübl, there was no point dealing with them in order
because there was only one Oranienstübl.'

Anyone who was looking for commercial premises would
queue up to see her, and she aimed to treat small tradespeople every bit as well as people with plans to promote
culture in Mitte. The culture department soon began sending artists looking for studios directly to her. Jutta organized
joint appointments with Dolly Leupold, who was in charge
of decentralized cultural activities at the culture department, because, in her own words, two heads are better than
one. Some of the artists advised by Leupold and Weitz still
recall that they were never treated like supplicants. The two
women were masters in the art of making things happen, a
discipline that bureaucracies value far less than they ought
to.

Jutta started to put together her own portfolio of spaces
she could offer to artists searching for somewhere to work.

'I went to ask individual colleagues for properties they were finding difficult to rent out and collected all the descriptions together in a box', she says. 'That meant I was lucky enough to have a few properties even without my own administrative purview, and the administrators didn't get annoyed with me for treading on their toes.'

Jutta established a strategy of offering people in the cultural sphere spaces to use with a temporary licence. This wasn't appropriate for small tradespeople, but artists and nightclub managers were generally willing to make do with dilapidated buildings and run the risk of having their tenancy terminated with three months' notice. The ownership situation was often unclear, and family trusts would occasionally squabble over buildings. The temporary licence could run for several years, and sometimes the old or new proprietors did renew the tenancy agreement.

What Jutta was doing from her office at the WBM was silent urban development. Sometimes she would find rooms for various initiatives working in similar fields on the same street corner. These decisions were guided by a very simple consideration. 'It's nicer for an artist to have three other artists working nearby than to slog away on your own.'

The daily practice of creatively juggling temporary-licence agreements evolved into cultural policy work. She began arranging regular weekend breakfasts at her home to which she invited people from the creative sector. Her job had introduced her to an awful lot of people in Mitte working in culture, but often they didn't know one another. People filed in and out of her flat from dawn till dusk, occasionally joined by the councillors responsible for the economy or construction.

From time to time, when a problem cropped up at the Eimer, the police would ring Jutta's doorbell at night because she was officially in charge of such places for the housing association. Without authorization or mandate, she would devote her free time to her cultural work as well. She was sometimes out on the town for longer than she'd been while working at the Prater.

'My work took over my life. I would have found it impossible to separate it from my private life, and yet I simply wasn't prepared to view it as just a job', she says. Looking back, she thinks that her absorption in her work helped her through a time of unprecedented upheaval. 'Many political issues would definitely have made me feel more powerless and I'd have wrangled with the situation more if I hadn't had a sense of being able to go quietly about something that would have an impact.'

Most clubs in the early nineties were located in WBM buildings, quite simply because the WBM managed almost every building in Mitte. The rhythm of city centre life was defined by art and techno now.

Neues Forum was founded in September 1989 in East Germany. The group published a proclamation entitled 'The Time is Ripe – A New Beginning '89'. The document called for a public, democratic dialogue in the GDR about the functions of the constitutional state, the economy and the cultural sector, but contained no concrete political demands. Although the regime branded Neues Forum a hostile organization, 200,000 East German citizens had signed the appeal by the end of 1989. One of the signatories was Jutta Weitz because, in her opinion, there was no alternative. Only one other person at her workplace put their name to the petition. Although she would not describe herself as taking a stand, a sense of defiance had prevented her from joining the SED when she was asked to become a member.

'If I'd been asked at 19 if I wanted to join the party, I might well have said yes. Unfortunately, though, they asked me at

18 when I was going through a petulant phase, and I decided I didn't need to join an organization they were already in.'

Her parents were SED members, and her grandfather had been an active communist during the Nazi regime. Jutta signed the Neues Forum appeal because she thought it was reasonable. Neues Forum had been the mainstay of the demonstrations of autumn 1989, but in December it opposed the premature reunification of the two German states. According to Neues Forum's analysis, this would create a quick route to prosperity for some while bringing unemployment, little say and rent hikes for the many, as well as legalizing extreme right-wing parties and neo-fascist organizations.

Jutta was promoted to deputy director of the commercial premises department. Anyone else would have been delighted, but Jutta found it problematic. 'It was clear to me that I couldn't stay there. I didn't think it was right.'

Being deputy head of department would have prevented her from being able to do what she always did when it came to artists, which was to bend the rules. She made sure they put her name in the bottom left-hand corner of the organizational chart 'where there was no one above or below me'. It's a nice image that tells you everything you need to know about her.

Even though one side effect of her work was that the cultural use of WBM's assets increased their value, Jutta lived with the constant threat of being called to account and always took care to balance the books in her limited area of activity. On the other hand, her motto was that artists who used the housing association's buildings under licence were not required to generate a profit, just cause no economic damage. Her bosses let her get on with it, although they made it clear that they didn't want any trouble. This arrangement worked for a long time, but it was always going to be a temporary state of affairs. Jutta Weitz now works with Dolly Leupold for a charity called Förderband or 'Conveyor Belt'.

Towards the end of her time at the WBM, Jutta became conscious of how much the times had changed. Now young people who were still at school would turn up to see her with a fully fledged business idea they wanted to put into practice.

'The pressure is so much greater, and young people just don't have that breathing space any more. Creatives are continually urged to be profitable', she says.

WBM's cultural funding is now assessed in terms of its PR benefits.

3

Occupying the Government District

The night the Wall came down

On 9 November 1989 a few journalism students from the Freie Universität are sitting in a kitchen in Hobrechtstrasse. It may be the day our seminar group drafts a research paper on Roman Jakobson's theory of semiotics, but maybe not. When we've finished working, we have pasta for dinner. The radio announces that the Wall is open. Staring at one another in disbelief, we lay down our forks. The nearest border point we know is on Prinzenstrasse. Half an hour later, we're gazing into the stunned faces of GDR citizens crossing the border on foot or in Trabants. A cheering crowd has gathered to welcome the folks from East Berlin, some of whom are weeping. One West Berliner drums on the roof of every Trabant that drives across the former border between the sectors. A long-haired hippie from East Berlin in a parka comes up to us. He wants to visit some friends in West Berlin and hasn't a clue how to get to their place.

Thorsten Schilling had just under six months to study the spirit of West Berlin before it disappeared.

'West Berlin was still there in summer 1989. It began to fade away that November. People were wearing black shirts at the time. The eighties fashion was to be cool and aloof, like John Lurie in *Stranger than Paradise*. It was like that in Schöneberg, at Café M, and at the Madonna in Kreuzberg – loud music and everyone sitting there, smoking, saying nothing and looking earnest. Not long afterwards, blathering Ossis would be sitting in all the cool places in West Berlin, breaking all the conventions. The cool silence had given way to loud conversation, like the Chinese travelling around Europe on trains nowadays. For the first few weeks the Easterners were euphoric, liberated from the conventions that used to dictate how they behaved in public. They were much louder in the West than they would have been back home. On the underground people would ask, "Can you tell me where the Ku'damm[1] is? I'm from East Berlin!" Those were crazy times – the first shock to West Berlin's system.'

This shock manifested itself as masses of Easterners suddenly being able to move freely around Europe. The Wall was down, and the era of small, straightforward West Berlin was over. East German citizens were besieging the western half of the city. They went shopping in supermarkets with their welcome money, and snaking queues formed outside. The whole of Eastern Europe seemed to come together to do business at the Polish market in Gleisdreieck. The fall of the Wall was a greater shock for some people in West Berlin than it was for many East Germans. Some Westerners decided to move back to their sleepy southern university towns at the first opportunity, and many long-time West

[1] The Kurfürstendamm, referred to colloquially as Ku'damm, is one of Berlin's most famous avenues.

Berliners would have been quite satisfied with tasting life in the eastern part of the city just once. They stayed in their own part of town if they could help it. The Wall may not have been visible any more, but it hadn't gone away.

West-Berlin, Westberlin, Restberlin

When West Berlin was still a thing, most of its inhabitants called it West-Berlin. The sectors of the three Western allies were officially known as Berlin (West), which was intended to demonstrate that the whole of Berlin was subject to the authority of the four occupying powers. The comrades in the East, on the other hand, referred disrespectfully to 'Restberlin' – the rump of the city surrounded by their wall, the half of the city full of run-down late-nineteenth-century buildings and ugly fifties apartment blocks – as Westberlin. West Berliners and East Berliners had at least one thing in common: they couldn't walk around their city without sooner or later bumping into the Wall.

Near Sebastianstrasse in Kreuzberg, a kink in the Wall brought it so close to old buildings on the West Berlin side that it seemed as if a car might just about squeeze through. Mouldy mattresses lay in puddles on the street alongside other waste: it looked like the edge of civilization.

If a West Berliner decided to take the underground from Kreuzberg to Wedding, both in West Berlin, the journey resembled a ghost train. If they started their trip on line 6 at Mehringdamm, the train would stop in a few more stations in West Berlin, but from then on it jolted its way through dimly lit, eerily deserted stations in the East before recrossing the border into the West. By the time the traveller got out in Wedding again, they would have traversed the capital of the German Democratic Republic underground.

West Berlin was a place on life support. The money to fund this shining advert for the free world in the middle of the Eastern Bloc came from West Germany. Ever since Stalin's blockade of Berlin, the government of the Federal Republic had tempted people and businesses to West Berlin through a combination of tax breaks and measures to support investment and wages. Paradoxically, this merely added to the feeling that West Berlin was some sort of gilded cage. Civil servants would accept lower salaries to be transferred elsewhere in West Germany, and someone who had received funding to build a house or flat was required to pay it back when they left the city.

Entire areas of old buildings had been demolished since the sixties. Urban planners in the West and the East were united by the modernist idea of building soulless blocks for the working population, fitted with all mod cons and surrounded by grass. Building new neighbourhoods on the edge of the city proved a lucrative business for West Berlin construction companies and a boon for the city's notorious sleaze. The windfall of subsidized social housing fed corruption, but West Berlin politicians simply ramped up the anti-communist rhetoric to deflect attention.

'For decades after the war, Berlin's streets and squares were dominated by the triumphant signs on which the federal government and Berlin council bragged about "Demolishing to reconstruct!"', Wolf Jobst Siedler wrote. As a conservative, he was critical of the modernizing rebuilding schemes after the war. He could not be described as nostalgic for the Wilhelmine city, which he regarded as an aesthetic failure, and remarked that the only thing that could make you nostalgic for the old tenement buildings were the even greater failings of Berlin's post-war architecture. The partial destruction of some Wilhelmine buildings had given them a dignity they did not previously possess.

At least one of the reasons squatters moved into West Berlin's nineteenth-century neighbourhoods was this slash-and-burn redevelopment. They preferred to live in old houses in the middle of the city rather than on suburban estates and in satellite towns, and so they occupied spacious old flats with wooden floors and high ceilings where well-off families and army officers had once resided. The kitchens of some street-facing flats still contained the small chambers where the servants were once accommodated. The polit-rock band Ton Steine Scherben sang about the struggle against the clearance of the Georg von Rauch Haus in 1972, proclaiming, 'You'll never get us out / this is our house!' That song became the anthem of an entire movement. The squatters opened pubs, migrants opened shops, and gradually life returned to the old tenements.

Many West Germans viewed West Berlin as an unattractive city, an intermediate zone of which the best thing that could be said was that it had a morbid charm. Many young men moved here from West Germany to avoid military service. Berlin's largely negative reputation made it a good place to experiment. A diverse and often contradictory counterculture took hold, especially in Kreuzberg where green, alternative reformers set up self-administering companies, the hippie-dom of the early seventies was gradually replaced by punk, and hedonists of all sexual persuasions came together to party.

West Berlin was an urban melting pot of different life-styles and mentalities, a place with ample niches for lifestyles that deviated from the norm. You could live cheaply, you could party long and hard, and you could go out for break-fast at three in the morning. Bars were allowed to stay open all night.

West Berlin's status as a haven for all was not to everyone's liking. Many lower-middle-class residents of Lichtenrade, Lichterfelde and Lankwitz reckoned that anyone living in

Kreuzberg was a criminal, by which they meant long-haired people, punks, drug dealers, gays and left-wing anarchists. West Berlin's degradation by the Nazis from a metropolis to a provincial backwater had also left deep scars in its inhabitants' minds and in the architecture.

All these factors contributed to the fascination Berlin exerted on so many visitors. In the summer of 1976 David Bowie moved from Los Angeles to Berlin and set up home with his female assistant and his friend and fellow musician Iggy Pop in a flat at Hauptstrasse 155 in Schöneberg. In West Berlin Bowie was free to walk more or less wherever he liked without being recognized. He made trips into the eastern sector via Checkpoint Charlie on his constant quest to find places with some link to Hitler, whom he had provocatively referred to in one interview as one of the first rock stars. He and Iggy Pop toured the discos, bars and pubs of West Berlin.

Iggy celebrated their nightclubbing jaunts in his song of the same name, which the two stars recorded together in a studio at night. It's hard to tell if the song is a dark and scabrous ode to excess or a sarcastic self-portrait of people who've smoked too many cigarettes, snorted too much cocaine and not eaten enough fruit. 'We see people, brand new people / We learn dances, brand new dances', sings Iggy Pop. Which would sound exciting, were it not for the veil of emotional detachment and the absence of any vitality: 'We're an ice machine / We walk like a ghost.'

David Bowie went on to compose three albums and Iggy Pop two while they were in West Berlin, with some of the tracks recorded at one of Hansa's two studios on Potsdamer Platz – 'Recorded at Hansa by the Wall, Berlin.' Legend has it that East German border guards used to watch the musicians at work through their binoculars. The title song of Bowie's album 'Heroes' is about a couple of lovers by the

Wall, which the Sex Pistols had already immortalized in song: 'In Sensurround sound in a two-inch wall / Well I was waiting for the communist call / I didn't ask for sunshine, and I got World War Three / I'm looking over the wall and they're looking at me!' For punk romantics, Berlin stood for the polar opposite of a civilization in crisis – a crisis that could be countered only through individual, idiosyncratic initiative. Bowie puts the title 'Heroes' between quotation marks to signal an emotional distance from the pathos of a word that sounds even more toxic here in the Third Reich's former capital than it does elsewhere.

'Heroes' is also on the soundtrack to *Christiane F.*, the dramatic film about teenage junkies around Bahnhof Zoo in West Berlin, which lends a hint of glamour to the devastation of heroin addiction. While 'Heroes' plays, a gang of teenagers rampages through the Europa-Center shopping mall. They keep dropping to the ground as they run, as if they've been shot, then get back up and carry on running past the shop windows as Bowie sings, 'Though nothing / Will keep us together / We could steal time / Just for one day / We can be heroes / For ever and ever.'

In order to build the 100-metre-tall Europa-Center, the West Berlin businessman Karl Heinz Pepper had pulled together a few million Deutschmarks from rich West Germans. The building on Breitscheidplatz was completed in 1965 on the site where the Romanisches Café once stood. This meeting place of the artistic avant-garde during the Weimar Republic had sustained a direct hit during a bombing raid on 21 November 1943 and was gutted in the ensuing blaze. For a while the Europa-Center was the tallest building in West Berlin. Anyone investing in West Berlin was rewarded with tax breaks, and Chancellor Ludwig Erhard accused Pepper of 'gross abuse' of these preferential tax arrangements during its construction.

In the 1990s *Der Spiegel* concluded that 'this project was the first spectacular case of state-sponsored asset accumulation for the rich and the super-rich'. By then the area around the Kurfürstendamm was on the slide because new streams of tax-incentivized investment had started pouring into Mitte after the fall of the Wall. Office block after office block shot up into the sky. Many of these stood empty once completed, sending the price of office space into a nosedive. One by one, tenants deserted the Europa-Center, inspiring one West Berlin estate agent to suggest that it would be preferable to tear it down. The destruction of existing structures has been a constant theme throughout Berlin's history.

Whereas Iggy Pop and David Bowie's sojourn has long since entered the annals of pop, the Berlin years of transsexual punk icon Wayne County have almost passed into oblivion. Wayne County relished Berlin's backdrop of run-down nineteenth-century neighbourhoods, gleaming new buildings and bizarre bars. Wayne, who later changed his name to Jayne, had played his part in the invention of punk in New York City and had also influenced David Bowie. He arrived in Berlin in the late seventies. In 1979 he and his band The Electric Chairs recorded the song 'Berlin', which includes the lyrics: 'The buildings are brand new / There's a place for me and you / And a past that refuses to die.' There is no more succinct description of West Berlin than those three lines.

Jayne County accepted a role in Rosa von Praunheim's *Berlin Blues*, released in 1983 and featuring eight performers from the Berlin trans scene whom the director largely allowed to act themselves. Von Praunheim's film treats them with an acceptance they otherwise only encountered in the bars of West Berlin. German film critics proved incapable of recognizing this, detecting in this over-the-top cabaret film neither 'social realism' nor 'the experience of exclusion and helpless rage'. Sceptical critics from Munich and Cologne were not wrong to see *Berlin Blues* as a publicity clip for Berlin, where a few scattered bars and discos keep the memory of Berlin's pre-Nazi history as a pulsating, cosmopolitan metropolis alive. That is another element of the past that refuses to die, as Wayne County puts it in his Berlin song.

One of the islands of West Berlin subculture where everyone was welcome was Café Anfall, which opened in Kreuzberg's Gneisenaustrasse in the early eighties.

'It was an old Berlin bar, with a wooden counter, that had been taken over by members of the '68 generation. It had sofas – it was a slouchy kind of place. However, that all changed in the wake of the New Wave. I joined in its second year after coming to Berlin when I was nineteen. It must have been 1981. It was a collective. Two people took turns behind the bar, with one of us always in charge of the mix-tape. It was one of the first centres of the house scene, and before that it had been a punk place for a bit. It was a melting pot of partygoers with this punk vibe', Mari Lippok says. She kept a close eye on the evolving scene in the old West Berlin and new Mitte while working behind the counters of various bars, DJing or organizing parties. She later worked for *De:Bug*, a magazine for electronic lifestyles, founded in Mitte in the mid-nineties.

The Anfall had its heyday in the mid-1980s, when pop was going through an eclectic phase as punk and New Wave met hip-hop and house. The place was packed at weekends. People crowded into the Anfall's long narrow interior and clustered in bunches outside the entrance. Drag queens and trannies were regulars too. The best parties – and this was true both before and after the fall of the Wall – were the ones where gay men showed heterosexuals how to have fun. They were held in places like the Anfall where no one gave a damn about your sexual orientation or background.

'Our name said what we stood for ['Anfall' means 'fit' or 'seizure']', Mari Lippok says. 'There were all kinds of people there who got nicknames because we had no idea what they were really called. It would be unthinkable today that marginal figures and homeless people were welcome, that you go into a club and there'd be all these freaks there having a good time. By 1989 when the Wall came down, Café Anfall had long since crested the wave when champagne flowed like water and there was dancing on the tables. After that, it ebbed away slowly to the East.'

At first, not many people crossed the former zonal border on a night out. In conservative Kreuzberg, which was firmly in the grip of the muesli and punk brigade, the new trends from Mitte took years to arrive.

The members of a band called Fleischmann were regulars at Café Anfall, where the bartenders dubbed them the milky coffee brigade.

'I knew Gerriet Schultz when he came into Anfall and announced, "I've opened this place and we're throwing a big opening night party!" I can still remember him sitting there proudly, and then we went over there to have a look', Mari Lippok says.

Fleischmann were a four-man metal band who got together in 1989 in West Berlin. Two of its members were from the West, two from the East. They were looking for a rehearsal room. One of the young guys from the East knew a house that might be suitable, not far from Kreuzberg, just the other side of Checkpoint Charlie. It was the former Berlin flagship of the Württembergische Metallwarenfabrik Aktiengesellschaft, or WMF for short, a metalware company with its headquarters in a small south-west German town. The WMF building was on the corner of Mauerstrasse and Leipziger Strasse, once a prestigious address.

When the Wall came down, the WMF building housed

among other things a state-owned grocery shop and a few offices and retail spaces. The grocery shop on the ground floor stayed on for quite some time, but all the other tenants moved out of the building in the summer of 1990, leaving it spotlessly clean. After setting up their rehearsal room, Fleischmann soon squatted the fourth floor with some of their mates. Along with all the empty rooms, there was also a working telephone.

People founded a club in the cellar. Whenever there was a party in the building, people would say, 'Let's go to WMF!', and that's how the place got its name.

In the mouse hole: Stadtmitte underground station

Pit Schultz is standing in the mouse hole. That's the name of the tiled tunnel connecting the platforms of underground lines U2 and U6. Pit Schultz and his mate Daniel Pflumm have painted white the tunnel's wooden boards, which used to be covered with adverts. In black letters and pho-netic script they have painted on the boards the names of twenty-three cities of over two million inhabitants from all five continents. The name of only one city features twice: from whichever end of the tunnel you enter, the imaginary round-the-world trip begins in Berlin. The other names emblazoned along the sides as you change from one line onto the other include Kinshasa and Singapore, New York and Hong Kong, Buenos Aires and Warsaw. You sometimes have to look twice as you walk along the 160-metre-long tunnel: the names of the cities seem foreign because they are not spelled in the usual way.

The appeal to passers-by to say the names of Kinshasa or Warsaw aloud is not without irony, given that so few travellers with the Berlin Transport Authority or BVG are

heading off on, or returning from, an intercontinental journey. All they want to do is change from the U6 onto the U2
or vice versa. The mouse hole has only been reopened since
the summer of 1990 brought monetary union and the reunification of the West and East Berlin underground systems.
Now the U6 trains stop at the ghost stations in the East too.

Pit Schultz is dressed in jeans and a T-shirt and has
shoulder-length hair. He leans against one of the two Berlin
boards with studied nonchalance as he speaks to the camera.
'It's about shaping our surroundings – neither to leave everything exactly as it is nor to let any advertising in here. It's
about making a difference, an aesthetic difference.'

The editor grants Pit three short sentences at the beginning of a TV report broadcast on Sender Freies Berlin in
September 1989. Pit Schultz and Daniel Pflumm's mouse-
hole project serves to introduce viewers to a new place that
the TV station has discovered – 'the Bermuda triangle of
cultural squatters between Leipziger Strasse, Kronenstrasse
and Mauerstrasse', as the SFB reporter explains off-camera.
Pit Schultz is one of these cultural squatters, the 'Bermuda
triangle' a slightly lurid but nevertheless fitting name for the
place featured in the report.

At the western end of the block between Friedrichstrasse,
Leipziger Strasse, Kronenstrasse and Mauerstrasse, three
buildings are still standing. The WMF house is on the
corner of Leipziger Strasse and Mauerstrasse, a vacant plot
separating it from Mauerstrasse 15. There's a further gaping,
empty site on the corner of Mauerstrasse and Kronenstrasse,
in the middle of which stands a staghorn sumac tree that
has grown to a considerable height. Last but not least, the
house at Kronenstrasse 3 marks the northernmost point of
the 'Bermuda triangle'. Several of the adjacent buildings are
missing, and the houses in their back courtyards have also
vanished. In GDR times, only a few huts were erected on

Fig. 9 The WMF building on the corner of Leipziger Strasse and
Mauerstrasse. The picture was taken on 2 July 1990

this large vacant site. Standing next to Kronenstrasse 3 at
the tip of the triangle, you can look out over a wide-open
space stretching to Leipziger Strasse, which is the southern
boundary of what used to be a block. Stadtmitte underground station is on its eastern side.

It is here that Pit Schultz stands in front of the camera
and makes clear in his three allotted sentences that the
art scene is staking a claim to the old city centre. Pit is a
member of the Botschaft, which is the name the fourth-
floor squatters connected to Fleischmann have chosen for

their group. The word 'Botschaft' has two meanings: 'message' and 'embassy'. Both Checkpoint Charlie, the erstwhile GDR border crossing for diplomats, and Wilhelmstrasse are within a stone's throw of here. From the days of the German Empire to the early morning of 2 May 1945 when General Helmuth Weidling signed the capitulation, thereby surrendering the city to the Red Army, Wilhelmstrasse has been synonymous with the seat of government. A large number of foreign embassies have traditionally been located in the government quarter around this street. In the GDR era, the Czechoslovak Socialist Republic, Hungary and North Korea all built new embassies near the WMF building. Until the fall of the Wall, the WMF building itself hosted the showrooms of the state-owned domestic and international public utility company, Versina, where visitors could view samples of the available products while sitting sedately on couches and in armchairs. Versina supplied goods to accredited foreign diplomatic missions in East Germany as well as East German embassies abroad.

So the Botschaft seems an appropriate name for a group comprising four artists, four film studies students, one computer science student, two musicians, an electrical engineer and a conservator. The first event arranged by their association, Botschaft e.V., is held on the same day Mainzer Strasse is cleared. Shortly afterwards, Botschaft organizes an event called 'Dromomania – The Cult and Rituals of Everyday Mobility', prompted by the Senate's plans to expand Leipziger Strasse to three lanes in each direction, which has already been forced through by the SED government. The desired objective of making Potsdamer Platz accessible by car threatens the WMF building with demolition. The East German state had already forcibly evicted the occupants in 1986 for this precise purpose. Two months after 'Dromomania', the building is listed.

'Dromomania' lasts for five days. The WMF building hosts art happenings, discussions and events about urban planning, traffic and the history and future of Berlin-Mitte. The '9th December' group, a coalition of urban planners from East and West, presents its 'Charter for the Middle of Berlin'. It advocates functional and social mixed use of the future city centre and for the planning process to take account of the history of the war and of the construction of the Wall. At the Botschaft's premises, traffic calming measures are explained while the noise of the traffic at the junction of Leipziger Strasse and Mauerstrasse is recorded, mixed live with beats and other sounds and then replayed to the cars waiting at the traffic lights.

Part of the 'Dromomania' programme involves a conversation with five elderly women who recall how the area around Potsdamer Platz used to be. One of the old ladies spent the final years of the war, when she was a student, in the WMF building, where the armaments company Rheinmetall-Borsig was using computers invented by Konrad Zuse to calculate the trajectories of a missile, presumably the F-55 air-defence missile, code name 'Fire Lily'. Female students called up for auxiliary service had to report for duty at 4:30 in the morning to an office that was not heated, to prevent them from dozing off. They calculated the coordinates of a flight path and entered them into tables without having the slightest inkling of the purpose of this work. These young women worked sixty hours per week and, due to the bombing raids, kept having to go down into the cellar for the night. The WMF students were in the WMF building on 3 February 1945 when the top floor was hit and obliterated by a phosphorous firebomb. That was the day Berlin-Mitte was reduced to the state in which it was still to be found after the fall of the Wall.

That Saturday, 3 February 1945, 939 bombers from the United States Army Air Forces (USAAF) infiltrate Berlin's air space. The early warning is sounded at 10:27, and the air-raid siren starts blaring at 10:39. It is the 288th air-raid alert since the beginning of the war. Then the bombs begin to fall. Berlin's anti-air-raid headquarters announces in its 240th 'Report on Air Raids on the Capital of the Reich' five days later that massed squadrons of American fighters and bombers attacked the capital in the morning when the sky was clear.

> Some 700 to 800 aircraft flew over the city in four waves, releasing a large number of explosive bombs and firebombs, most of them at high density. According to present reports, approximately 4,000 explosive bombs, 150,000 incendiary sticks and 500 liquid bombs were dropped. The raid was concentrated on the area within the urban circular railway, with the districts of Kreuzberg, Mitte, Horst Wessel and Wedding worst affected,

runs the announcement. (The Horst Wessel district of the city reverted to its original name of Friedrichshain at the end of the war.)

The report's conclusion for Mitte district reads as follows:

> Badly hit across the board. The areas affected by particularly dense carpet-bombing stretch in a broad swathe from the south-western corner of the district (Potsdamer Platz – Leipziger Platz – Hermann Göring Strasse – Melchiorstrasse) in a north-easterly direction to the area around Bahnhof Alexanderplatz but also branching off towards the north-west (Stettiner Bahnhof area) and the south-east (Köpenicker Strasse and Melchiorstrasse areas).

The number of casualties is later estimated at 2,894 dead, 20,000 injured and 120,000 made homeless as a result of the air raid.

The anti-air-raid headquarters is under the authority of the city mayor of Berlin. Their reports are marked
'Confidential! For internal use only!' and are distributed to
a relatively small number of recipients. Neither the enemy's
bomber command nor the local population are to learn
any details about which areas have been hit and how much
damage has been done. By now Berliners have lost count of
the number of nights they have spent in shelters. The Führer
has long since lost all desire to see the bomb damage his capital has sustained and is chauffeured through the city behind
drawn curtains. The bombers have been flying regular raids
since 1943 – USAAF aircraft by day, the British Royal Air
Force's Bomber Command by night.

The *Völkischer Beobachter* newspaper hails the bombing as
a blessing in urban development terms. Carl Fluhme writes
in January 1944 that the 'Jewish plutocracy' was endeavour-
ing to exterminate 'German socialism' but that the terror
bombing was having precisely the opposite effect. 'Every
building it destroys in Germany adds a stone to the tomb the
British and the Americans are preparing for their system of
exploitation. Every splintered chimney that rears up into the
sky from the smouldering ruins is a symbol of the collapse of
capitalism.' The terror bombing was clearing the 'contaminated ground' for 'healthy, practical and beautiful socialist
structures', the newspaper said.

This militant Nazi paper's appreciation of the bombard-
ments' contribution to urban planning and housing policy
was not entirely propaganda. Albert Speer had already
begun to prepare large expanses of land for his new Berlin.
Adolf Hitler and his friend Speer longed to turn the capital
of the Reich into the capital of the world, to be known as
'Germania'. Hitler had appointed Speer 'General Building
Inspector for the Reich Capital' in 1937. Speer planned to
drive two broad avenues through the city and build four

ring roads with, at their centre, a gigantic 'Great Hall'. This required the demolition of 52,144 apartments and the razing of entire neighbourhoods. To provide replacement flats for the tenants of the buildings that were to make way for Germania, Speer gave the order in 1938 that Jewish tenants were to be forcibly evicted, their assets confiscated and their property 'Aryanized'. The deportation of Jewish Berliners began three years later at Speer's behest; he was determined to stick to his timetable and clear the areas earmarked for demolition. Meanwhile, Speer had also been promoted to Minister of Armaments and ordered Auschwitz's transformation into the hub of a European slave market for German industry.

The objective of the air raid on 3 February 1945 is to support the Russian advance in the East by causing massive disruption to the economy of the capital of the Third Reich. Attacking the city centre deviates from the American doctrine of strategic bombing, which involves precision strikes on militarily relevant targets. US air raids could not be less surgical, however. A conference held in March 1945 to discuss the accuracy of the bombing establishes that the Eighth Air Force's success rate the previous winter was uncommonly low when the cloud cover was thick: 42 per cent of the bombs fell more than five miles from their intended targets. The US Air Force's 'precision strikes' are in fact akin to carpet-bombing.

By the autumn of 1944, not only have the Americans become extremely pessimistic about a quick end to the war, they also fear that the fighting might last far into the summer of 1945 if the Rhine is not crossed by 1 April and if the Soviet offensive gets bogged down in Poland. Their frustration at the slow progress of the war, combined with mounting casualties, increases the Americans' willingness at least to factor in the psychological effect of bombing on the enemy when planning air raids. Lieutenant General James Doolittle, the commander of the Eighth Air Force, advocates the selective bombing of industrial targets, but he is unable to win over his superiors.

The weather is good that morning, and the carpet-bombing of the city centre so dense that it unleashes a firestorm. It reduces everything in its path to ashes as it spreads east from the south of Friedrichstadt to the north-west of adjoining Luisenstadt until canals, parks and wide boulevards prevent it from sparking blazes in further parts of town. The fire burns for four days solid. It goes down as the most devastating of all the 363 recorded air raids on Berlin. Many churches and other historic build-ings in Mitte, Kreuzberg, Friedrichshain and Wedding are destroyed. The Reich Chancellery, the Party Chancellery, Gestapo headquarters and the Volksgerichtshof are hit, killing the so-called People's Court's notorious president, Roland Freisler. Bombs destroy two of Berlin's mainline railway stations, Anhalter Bahnhof and Potsdamer Bahnhof, though the latter has been out of action since taking a direct hit the previous year. The urban railway system is unaffected. Many of the vacant sites that continue to char-acterize the landscape of Mitte for some time after the fall of the Wall date from that morning. Anything left standing in the 'Bermuda triangle' around the WMF building after 3 February 1945 was subsequently demolished by the East German state. A large, empty wasteland gapes in the middle of the city, in direct proximity to the old and future govern-ment districts.

When the Wall comes down, this empty plot offers a reminder of the bombs, but there is nothing to mark the fact that this spot on the corner of Mauerstrasse and Kronenstrasse was the heart of the former capital of the Third Reich. At the junction of Kronenstrasse and Mauerstrasse there used to be the Dreifaltigkeitskirche where Schleiermacher once preached and Otto von Bismarck was confirmed. The Gestapo established their headquarters in the crypt of the bombed-out church in the final weeks of the war.

Its former outline is now marked by a series of coloured stones inserted into the road surface. Directly next door is the North Korean embassy, which has rented out part of its compound to the City Hostel. Every Saturday, you can watch the embassy staff gather in lines to sweep the court-yard. At the end of the war, here stood what remained of the Hotel Kaiserhof, where Hitler booked rooms for himself and his staff on 3 February 1931 and stayed until he was sworn in as chancellor. When it was time for the ceremony, he was driven two hundred metres to the Reich Chancellery.

Nothing remains of either the old or the new Reich Chancellery in Wilhelmstrasse either. The East German government built a residential complex there in the eighties, which Berlin residents referred to as 'Nomenklatura Prefab'. Where the entrance to the New Reich Chancellery used to be, a Chinese restaurant has opened its doors to diners.

Hitler celebrates his last birthday on 20 April 1945 in the Führer's bunker. Early the next morning, American bombers fly the last strategic bombing raid against the city. Now that the air-raid alerts have finished, the Berliners begin to hear a different siren from in previous years: the Red Army has started shelling the centre of Berlin. Three days later, the underground has stopped running. On the evening of 1 May 1945, while Red Army soldiers are observing the public holiday, the staff of the New Reich Chancellery, led by SS-Brigadeführer Wilhelm Mohnke, attempt to break out of the besieged city centre. From 11 p.m., ten groups are to cross Wilhelmsplatz at half-hourly intervals and reach the underground shaft at Kaiserhof station. The plan is to get to Stadtmitte station, slip through the mouse hole to the lower platform and march north, avoiding the Red Army's strangle-hold around the government quarter. Mohnke is guiding the first group made up of twenty men and four women, Hitler's secretaries and his dietician. They find their way through the mouse hole and advance slowly northwards along the dark tunnel until they can go no farther.

'We were prepared for the Russians but not for the BVG public transport authority', Mohnke tells the journalists James O'Donnell and Uwe Bahnsen in the summer of 1974. One hundred metres from the end of the platform of Friedrichstrasse station, the group runs into an iron bulkhead guarded by two BVG men. They refuse to obey Mohnke's order to open the bulkhead. 'They informed us with great officiousness that the bulkhead was closed every evening after the passage of the last train to protect the tunnel from flooding – we were directly under the river Spree. Even though there were no trains running, they said that they had to obey instructions.'

SS-Brigadeführer Mohnke turns back. Reflecting on it later, he still can't come up with a rational explanation for his decision. 'We were accustomed as soldiers to think in terms of orders and obedience. In this case, the instruction – even though it was "only" from the BVG – was that the bulkhead had to remain closed, and we heeded it.'

The breakout from the Führer's bunker was incorporated into the great tale of the 'downfall' which Joachim Fest recounts in his book *Inside Hitler's Bunker: The Last Days of the Third Reich*, and into its film adaptation, *Downfall*, by Bernd Eichinger. Neither Fest nor Eichinger relate the encounter between uniformed men in that U6 underground tunnel; it doesn't fit with what Fest describes as one of 'the most exciting events in German history'. It shows the banal side of a disaster where orders are given and obeyed to the bitter end.

Just under half a century later, the SFB TV crew leaves the mouse hole in Stadtmitte underground station and turns its attention to the building next door to WMF.

'The building at Mauerstrasse 15 was a brothel until the end of the war and has been a squat for the past year and a half. Twenty or so people from ten different countries work and live here', the reporter explains.

A young man says, 'Most of the people living here are artists. We'd like to offer a place where people from other countries can stay and we want to clean up the building.'

A second man adds, 'The most important thing is for them to give us a skip so we can take out all the rubbish. We really don't want to be living with rats.'

The reporter asks if there are rats around.

'I think so', the man replies.

A fly-tip behind the house has grown into a small hillock. It is being used as a backdrop for a play set in the immediate post-war years when many of the buildings in this particular block were still heaps of rubble. Lukas Taido Velvet, a student, is directing *Hotel Viktoria* at Mauerstrasse 15, which is what has drawn the film crew to the 'Bermuda triangle' this weekend. Viktoria is a fictional name. The first hotel and guest house at Mauerstrasse 15, mentioned in the 1929 Berlin address book, was run by Wanda Klopp. Seven years later, the hotel was registered as Pension Mellin. It was rechristened Hotel Clou in 1939, and that name stuck until a few years after the war.

The reporter says, 'Over three weekends, seventy-five actors will reconstruct the story of the building at Mauerstrasse 15. It isn't entirely accurate but it is very good, with cabbage soup for the audience and brawling on the brothel's balconies.'

Open arcades connect the building's short wings to one another on three floors, and on them actors are now performing short sketches dressed up as American and Russian officers and whores.

'It was a story about power struggles in a building that used to be a brothel. In parallel, they set up this replica black market around the building, complete with horse-drawn carts and police raids. Out of the blue, you'd have someone standing next to you, saying, "Want to barter?" and showing you a pocketful of hidden cutlery', Jutta Weitz recalls.

The triangle near Stadtmitte underground station developed into one of the cultural centres of Mitte. The Favela, an unusual bar serving caipirinhas, opened in the basement of the building at Mauerstrasse 15. It was joined in 1992 by the Elektro, which soon hosted Berlin's smallest techno club in a former electrical store just upstairs.

When the people from the Botschaft were forced to leave the WMF building, Jutta Weitz sorted out a floor for them

Fig. 10 The Friseur at Kronenstrasse 3 in August 1995

at Kronenstrasse 3 diagonally opposite, which also housed the office of the Chaos Computer Club. The Botschaft folks converted a former hairdressing salon on the ground floor of the building for their purposes.

Here, the charity, now staffed by a few people on temporary state-subsidized contracts, organized exhibitions and film festivals. At the Friseur, conceptual artists met documentary film-makers and party animals, and the Botschaft borrowed the round-table approach. For several years the only form of structure the charity had was a general meeting every Monday. The group had no spokesperson. In November 1993 the Botschaft inaugurated an exhibition called 'IG Farben – One Stock's Performance', which shed light on the activities of IG Farben, once the largest industrial conglomerate in Europe. Twenty-three of the company's senior executives were prosecuted at the Nuremberg trials for having set up the company's own concentration camp, employing hundreds of thousands of slave labourers and producing Zyklon B, the toxic gas used in the gas chambers. Despite having been in liquidation for decades, IG Farben's shares were still traded on the stock exchange and their value surged after the fall of the Wall because the firm was laying claim to fifty-four plots of land in Berlin, some of them in the government quarter.

The Botschaft pasted posters to the buildings claimed by IG Farben and invited Hans Frankenthal to the inauguration of the exhibition in the Friseur. As a young man, Frankenthal had been one of the company's forced labourers at Auschwitz-Monowitz. He told slightly more than a dozen people who had gathered that Friday evening that only quick thinking had ensured that he had been able to work at the Buna-Werke factory. When ordered to give his age on the ramp at Auschwitz, he said that he was twenty-one rather than sixteen because he had noticed that his peers were being sent over to stand with the elderly and the children.

Hans Frankenthal tried his best to sabotage production in Monowitz.

The events organized by the Botschaft in the early nineties demonstrated that theory, partying, political activism and local engagement didn't have to be mutually exclusive. Their refusal to take part in the Documenta contemporary art exhibition in Kassel was legendary and, for some, still hard to believe. The Botschaft left behind a small archive of videos, brochures and strategy papers, all challenging the capitalist diktat of production for profit.

The Botschaft collective's activities dominated the Friseur's programme for two years. Subsequently, the trend turned increasingly to partying, with various committees taking responsibility for individual nights. At the heart of the diverse and ever-multiplying Friseur universe were Petra Trojan and Dominique Croissier, who served at the bar themselves underneath a photo of the actress Inge Meysel, who'd had her hair cut here before the Wall was built. At some point Petra gifted it to some Irish guests. These two women kept the Friseur running until the end because they could do what they liked there, even if it meant that they saw little else of Berlin beyond the four walls of the Friseur. They still marvel at how many people felt at home there.

'We became famous because no one paid for drinks', Petra remarks twenty years later. Many free drinks were poured at the Friseur, WMF and the Elektro. Either you were friends with the people behind the bar or you did something useful that entitled you to free beers.

A community of squatters

The story of Klaus Fahnert's book table under the awning of Serdar Yildirim's old news stand at Oranienburger Tor can also be traced back to the triangle formed by WMF, the Elektro and the Friseur. Klaus's face was weathered by the sun, wind and rain. Not much of it was visible, mind: it was obscured by greyish-white curls, bushy eyebrows and a rampant beard. Klaus's clothes weren't tattered or dirty, just a little too conspicuously threadbare for him to be an ordinary flat-dweller. This is what he used to look like as he stood in a corner of the Elektro, leaning against the bar with a beer in his hand and a smile that seemed slightly childish for a man in his forties. He was known as 'Hausklaus' in the Elektro, probably because he was always there.

'Hausklaus would always turn up with something', Daniel Pflumm says. 'The kind of things they sell at flea markets – or don't. Klaus kept finding things in skips and he'd bring them along to the Elektro. He didn't have any money but he'd still want a beer. He used to pay with weird little boxes, recorders or books he'd come across on one of his tours. One time, he brought a plastic children's piano. Klaus's offerings would pile up behind the bar. Sooner or later, he started getting his pints free. Anything to stop him paying!'

Klaus Fahnert lived at Mauerstrasse 15. And so did Slavian Stefanoski, nicknamed Slavko, for a few years.

'Yeah, Klaus was there. Santa Klaus', he says. 'Klaus was literally like Santa because he collected junk from the huge quantities lying around in Mitte. Our attic was full of stuff. All of it usable, but just old. Klaus lived in the attic. We would have a coffee together in the mornings. Black, no sugar. It was the best – a matter of taste. Klaus was a former psychiatric patient, with a very peculiar past, and there were other strange people like him in Mauerstrasse.'

Slavko Stefanoski recalls a gay man, the son of a German mother and a black US soldier, who dressed as a woman. 'He was a very nice guy, but unfortunately he introduced heroin to Mauerstrasse. There were dark sides to living in that building too. The heroin thing was bad. Others had a cocaine habit, which later spread to Tacheles.'

Almost a year passes before Slavko Stefanoski finally pops up on my computer via Skype to talk to me about his years at Mauerstrasse 15. We've exchanged a few mails, then texted back and forth after he got hold of a mobile phone. After a while everything's sorted, and his face appears, slightly pixelated, on my screen. Tanned, with shoulder-length hair, he sits there in his home town of Ohrid in Macedonia and explains to me why skyping didn't work during the winter.

'There are no visitors here in winter. I hardly earn anything. I survive. In summer everything relaxes again. I do edutainment six months a year, guiding people around the town, nattering away to tourists, and they pay me for it. I'm a philosopher, so I have a lot to say and visitors like that. Getting through the summer has its problems too. I met these four girls from Italy yesterday and we hung out together, eating and drinking. Drinking far too much. That's the trouble with tourism. There was this graffiti in Tacheles that read, "Tourism is terrorism." That's what we experienced as squatters, all these visitors disturbing us. I was terrorized by those four Italian girls yesterday. I'm not complaining. My work always involves preaching now. I try to communicate the Christian meaning of life. Everything is love, everything's fine, and everything will be fine. I met a girl back then on the grass on the corner of Kronenstrasse and Mauerstrasse. She was handing out pieces of paper with the words "Everything will be fine" on them. Nothing more. I liked that.'

When Slavko Stefanoski was growing up in Ohrid, Macedonia was part of Yugoslavia. He broke off his studies in 1987, went travelling and visited Germany for the first time. He visited some friends in Kreuzberg from whose flat he could see the Wall. Those travels were the beginning of what he calls his squatter life.

'I've done a lot of squatting since then, and I just can't kick the habit.' He could tell lots of stories about squatting in London, Paris, Berlin, Spain and Italy. 'Squatting is an old tradition in northern Europe, whereas in southern Europe it's new, an adventure. Property is sacred in the south, so it's a war. It's crazy what goes down when you occupy a building. Squatting's practical, but it's also a discourse on how to live, how to imagine urban living, how the city emerges and how you can shape it.'

Slavko travelled from one squat to the next. In 1990 he returned to Berlin and found a job in Moabit in the former western half of the city.

'That was immediately after the fall of the Wall, and obviously I often went to Mitte because there was lots going on. I was already familiar with the building at Mauerstrasse 15, which was squatted shortly after the Wende. On that corner were the Friseur and WMF and between them was this mad house full of interesting people at Mauerstrasse 15. I went there a lot, but I was also at Tacheles a lot. I was permanently patrolling squats all over Berlin.'

The civil war in Yugoslavia erupted a year later. Though far from home, the war was constantly on Slavko's mind. 'I was sick of Europe. That autumn I headed to Africa and crossed the Sahara.'

Slavko spent that winter in Africa, then travelled around Europe and through the battlegrounds of the Yugoslavian civil war, and spent the following winter in Ohrid. After that, he went back to Berlin and moved into Mauerstrasse 15.

'I didn't feel like working any more and I no longer wanted to be an occasional squatter – I wanted to be part of the squatting movement. Also, I didn't have a flat and I needed to find somewhere. There were other places to live, of course, but I wanted to be in Mauerstrasse because I knew the place from earlier. It was a very unassuming building. It had once been a hotel and I'd been told it was also a brothel.'

The Mauerstrasse squatters made ends meet by washing the windows of cars forced to stop at the traffic lights.

'That's how the whole Mauerhaus kept their heads above water', Slavko says. That junction is supposedly where the whole car-window-cleaning business in Berlin started. 'I'd seen them do it in London. It's logical: there are lots of people driving through, and you can earn some money. Being a squatter means often being pretty broke. We didn't work much. The best thing about living in that building in Mauerstrasse was doing nothing. Being free, not paying taxes or rent or for the electricity, but simply getting hold of the things you needed to make it through the day – food and tobacco. If you had a little extra, then that was fantastic.'

Mauerstrasse 15 wasn't as well organized as other buildings squatted by the kids of intellectuals. Raquel Eulate found a place to live in the next-door WMF building after leaving a squat in Invalidenstrasse because she found it too cramped.

'I knew people living on the second floor, and they asked me if I fancied moving in. Not everyone in the building was very pleased. The art students there thought I was weird: they'd never met anyone like me before. The Botschaft people were a bit strict. But up on the second floor were some friends of Tom and Gerriet, who ran the WMF club in the cellar.' When the squatters were evicted from the WMF building, Raquel and a friend moved into the adjacent building, Mauerstrasse 15, where two second-floor rooms were free. 'I lived there until I got kicked out after six months.'

One day she came home to find her room occupied. Her belongings had been thrown onto the rubbish heap at the back of the building, although some of her other housemates had gathered some of it up again and kept it for her.

'I think a Mexican woman had just moved into the house. She thought I was too middle-class, like "The woman's got a job, so she doesn't need to live here." I'd worked maybe six times that year, earned a little bit of money, and they immediately started thinking I was rich. I thought there was no point in getting worked up about it, so I moved on. There was room elsewhere', Raquel says.

In next to no time people had declared her mad and too bourgeois. Anarchy doesn't mean there are no rules.

Anarchy had its positive sides in Daniel Pflumm's building. 'There was a plenary session once a month in Mauerstrasse 15. People would muck around beforehand and we tried to smoke as many joints as possible. We did discuss a few items, such as the water supply, but it never got any further than that. That was a plenary meeting! I didn't mind. I'd come more or less straight from squats in West Berlin, which was terrible because it was all about peer pressure, distinguishing between who would negotiate and who wouldn't.'

Daniel noticed the building at Mauerstrasse 15 soon after the Wall fell. 'On a first walk, a friend and I went from one hole in the Wall to the next, exploring the deepest, darkest East. We saw the building and told each other we should make something of it. Then, my mate Marc was looking for a flat. We walked past the place again, but the door was locked.'

Marc and Daniel shouted, and at long last a girl peered out of one of the middle windows by the balcony over the entrance. Anni, a punk of about twenty, was living there on her own.

Marc moved into Mauerstrasse 15 with his wife and two children.

'You wouldn't see that now – someone moving into a squat with his wife and children', Daniel says. 'I wonder why. The times haven't changed *that* much. The safety situation isn't much worse nowadays. Quite the opposite, in fact. You can live with two children in a tent on the street now.'

Marc worked in a local government cafeteria. He would bring leftover food home and put it out for everyone to share. Mauerstrasse 15 was not only a place to live, but a soup kitchen too. The food was delivered to their door and free.

'This guy who'd just got out of prison ended up there too. Misha told the best jokes. People came and went all the time, but Misha was a kind of mainstay. He wasn't the only one who was always there, but he was the father of the house. Anni lived there for a long time. Then she suddenly upped and left. One day she was just gone. After Marc also left, there wasn't the same sense of community any more. It became chaotic. Sooner or later, homeless people moved into the building. I've nothing against the homeless, it just wasn't a community any longer', Daniel says.

Some parts of the building dated back to the baroque phase in the city's expansion in the late seventeenth century. The building surrounded the courtyard in a horseshoe, with the short wings connected by an open gallery. The three walkways spanning the courtyard weren't particularly safe. Only the most basic repairs had been carried out since the end of the war, as the building had long been earmarked for demolition. Before the Wende it had been used by the committee advising the GDR's council of ministers.

The district architect, Eichhorst, wrote a letter to the construction department in October 1980, noting that new construction operations would probably make it necessary to demolish the building soon. 'The building's habitability and viability must of course be guaranteed until its demolition, but there should be no major investment exceeding that necessary to maintain its present condition.' The new construction operations never took place, and the building survived. The East German planners had greater success on the other side of the road, although the prefabricated residential block was only completed after the Wende.

Behind the house at Mauerstrasse 15 lie old mattresses, some broken white plastic chairs, blue rubbish bags, planks, car tyres, carpets, couches, folding chairs, rubble and rusty buckets. This riotous refuse dump keeps growing, because the city's street cleaners don't collect the rubbish from this building. At one time, the hill measures almost two metres at its highest point. You have to scramble over this heap to get to WMF, the club in the cellar of the former WMF building right next door. People traipse over this refuse dump every evening. But soon they don't queue for WMF any more, instead turning right to go down into the 'Sabor da Favela' – the 'Taste of the Favela'. People usually just refer to it as 'the Brazilian', because it's run by two young Brazilians.

'There was always a queue outside WMF. I imagine that the Brazilians figured it would be good business to open a caipirinha bar when the customers were already lining up outside', Raquel Eulate says. 'The Favela had only two small rooms at first, but business was so good that they expanded and kept refining the decor.' Soon, there are additional small booths with a single table in each.

If you're going to the Brazilian, you have to climb through an oval hole in the back of the building. However, even when you've found the courtyard, scaled the rubbish mountain, ignored the sign saying 'Private! No trespassing!' and squeezed through the opening, you're still only halfway through your rite of passage. The easily spooked – and, now and again, there's always one – have absolutely no desire to clamber down the banister-less stairs, by the dim glow of a few small candles, into the darkness. The Brazilian isn't for the claustrophobic, as the staircase is clogged with stacks of empty rum bottles.

'We always joked that we'd all die if there was a fire. There was no second exit', says Raquel, who lived in the house for a while. Favela epitomizes what bars in Mitte are all about. More than entertainment: adventure.

There are raffia breadbaskets for lampshades and white-washed walls. There's the odd stretch of wallpaper, but the rising damp means it has to be tacked onto the wall. It's decorated with jute bags and empty bottles of rum. The floor is carpeted with offcuts. All the furniture was picked up in the streets, and no two chairs are alike.

'It's all a bit makeshift, just like in a favela', one of the two Brazilians who run it tells a reporter.

The excited journalist says, 'Nowhere else in Berlin is there a place like this that radiates friendliness and such a mellow atmosphere.'

Ralf and Marcus opened this joint in September 1991. Rumour has it they studied in Moscow on scholarships provided by the Brazilian Communist Party. No one really knows how they ended up in Berlin.

'They told me they wanted to take a look at Berlin after the Wall came down. Then they must have stayed on, like everyone else', says Raquel.

Ralf and Marcus initially ran the Favela as a restaurant, but the cellar was later turned into a club where the only food was cachaça-filled coconuts and pineapples. Aside from the extravagant surroundings, which very few places in Berlin could rival, Favela was beer-free on principle and famous for its caipirinhas. Nowhere else in town served this Brazilian drink, made from cachaça, sugar, crushed ice and pounded limes, before Favela. Starting at the small bar in the corner, caipirinhas conquered the bars and clubs of Mitte within a couple of years and spread from there to the rest of

Fig. 11 Entrance to the Favela behind Mauerstrasse 15

the city. The major advantage for the restaurant owners was that caipirinhas yielded a tidy profit, despite being relatively labour-intensive to prepare. You had to cut limes and crush large quantities of ice. Slavko Stefanoski also worked in the basement bar for a time, 'pounding' ice for caipirinhas, as he puts it. At first, ice was in short supply at the Brazilian, as in most places in Mitte without an alcohol licence, most of which fetched their ice from McDonald's in the West. Initially, there was only one ice cube in each drink at the Brazilian. 'Otherwise, there'll be none left for anyone else', customers are warned.

Daniel Pflumm, who opened his own joint on the ground floor of Mauerstrasse 15 a year after Favela started up, only ever drank a couple of caipirinhas in that cellar. Daniel's Elektro was bang upstairs from the Favela. 'At opening time at the Elektro you were hit by the smell of caipirinha, so I went off them pretty quickly. The Brazilians were nice, and it was me who told them, "What? Caipirinhas for one mark fifty? You've got to double the price to turn a profit." They did, and the business ran like a dream.'

Although the price of a caipirinha rose steadily after that, no one had any complaints about the drinks, which were very strong. Drink more than two caipirinhas at the Favela and you struggled to make it back up the steep stairs. In the morning there would often be a few drunk people who hadn't made it home, sprawled on the rubbish heap behind the house.

The two Brazilians were poor when they opened the Favela. Soon, though, physics student Marcus would park his second-hand metallic-mauve Mercedes outside the Favela.

'The Brazilian bar was a gold mine', says Slavko, who lived on the fourth floor of the squat above. 'They didn't make much of a profit from the whole thing, though. What did they do with all the money? They spent it. I saw Marcus and

Ralf as artists. They did what they did to make money, sure, but it was also live art.'

By the time *Vogue* reported that the Favela was the hippest place in Berlin and an insider's tip for cocktails, the joint was buzzing at weekends. Now Jaguars from Düsseldorf would draw up in front of the building at night. Men helped their high-heeled companions over the rubbish heap.

Not that this spoiled the atmosphere: everybody was welcome at Favela. While Mauerstrasse 15 still had a mains electricity connection, they played salsa and bossa nova on cassette tapes. Sometimes there were live gigs, which became the rule when the power was cut off.

'People would often play the drums and other instruments', Slavko recalls.

Thorsten Schilling liked the Favela too. 'I loved it because it was so hot. You didn't sit down; you were standing the whole time in this dimly lit place. That's how it was in Mitte: you stood up in pubs and bars, you didn't sit down. In Prenzlauer Berg people would typically be seated, with candles on the tables – the epitome of the uptight, petit bourgeois mentality. We grew up in a culture where everyone stands and smokes. It's clearly better to stand. You can move around and chat to people. There are no surprises when you sit down. When you stand, though, glances flash back and forth. It's cramped in the Favela, so people touch and something happens. You could dance a bit, under no pressure, in a corner of the cellar. It was pretty dark.'

For four years, people partied at the Favela without any bother from the authorities, though journalists did break Mitte's unwritten rule: don't write about the Mitte bars you like to frequent, especially when things going on there are in breach of bye-laws or even the law. Just five years after it opened, the *taz* newspaper published an article about the

Brazilian, yet not without dropping a paradoxical hint that it'd be better to keep quiet about the joint:

> Otherwise, this might prompt the pernickety German authorities to ride into town even faster than they usually would, invading the still Wild East and driving out all the weird and wonderful night owls by the force of the law. Yet until that time, people can experience the full pleasure of clambering over heaps of rubbish and rubble to see out the hours of darkness in illegal dives and slum it in the friendliest of places. And *that* is surely the real attraction of the 'Bermuda triangle' between Mauerstrasse, Kronenstrasse and Leipziger Strasse.

In the bars, clubs and galleries of Mitte, workers and unemployed people mixed with professional slackers, and emerging artists talked to bohemians whose parents were professors, medium-sized entrepreneurs or managers.

Kriton Kalaitzidis, who helped organize the live music programme at the Friseur, can remember two special guests. 'There were two men who came on Thursday evenings, dressed up as rockers. They always wore leather jackets. I thought they were a bit weird, and so one night I asked Petra what kind of dudes they were. They'd always sit in the same corner, playing some game – chess, I think – and smoking one big, fat joint after another. They'd sit there quietly all evening. "They're cops," Petra said. "We're well protected." The Friseur was the place where they hung out. They met up every Thursday to play chess or draughts, smoke joints and drink their pints.'

By night Mitte seemed like the utopia of a classless society, but in the morning it looked very different. Then, some people would receive cheques from their parents or go to work for the authorities or agencies, while others stole food from supermarkets or scoured the streets for tables and chairs to furnish their flats.

'While some people were sleeping it off until the next party, other people you'd been dancing with the night before might already be buying the building where the last party had taken place', Natascha Sadr-Haghighian, one of the Botschaft brigade, wrote about the years following the fall of the Wall.

Thorsten Schilling has a similar view of the turn things took. 'We thought the squats and clubs were places of truth. That was the pathos of those days. Capitalism hadn't quite taken over yet, but the capitalists moved in as quickly as the squatters and the artists. The ensuing gentrification made the social fabric of Berlin much harsher. On the other hand, that's the great thing about a city like this: you're living in the same place, but you don't feel as if you're living in the same place, because there was a lot of upheaval and a far more radical turnover of people here than in other cities.'

Some of the people who vanished from Mitte swapped places with others against their will. One day, police officers turned up at Slavko Stefanoski's door and took him away.

'I was in a deportation centre for a fortnight, then they offered me a seat on a plane', Slavko says.

He has a ready answer for why his stay in the Federal Republic of Germany came to an end. 'Berlin was gradually morphing into the capital. I was no longer a squatter. There was no reason to keep me. The way the city was developing, there wasn't so much room for independent artists any more. I'm not complaining, just describing how things were.'

Slavko Stefanoski is still a squatter, and he's remained a traveller too. He cycled around the world between 2000 and 2002, starting in Ohrid and riding all the way to India, through China, over to America by ship and then back to Europe.

'A horse and a bike travel at the same speed. If you leave Europe in late summer and follow the sun and the coast at that god-given pace, you can sleep on the ground the whole time and the winter never catches up with you. The whole world is your home. You can do a spot of fishing, a bit of hunting, pick some vegetables and fruit. I was on the road for eighteen months.'

4

At the Elektro, Mauerstrasse 15

'Full Customer Satisfaction'

Someone has sprayed the word *DEPRECIATION* in black letters on the freshly painted wall of the corner house by the Landwehrkanal where Daniel Pflumm now lives. The building is on the edge of a neighbourhood that is getting more and more expensive. In 2012 the price per square metre of flats in certain parts of Neukölln rose to the levels observed in Mitte. The graffiti is a claim and a promise: it will depreciate the building's value. The same people who added the anti-real-estate slogan to the side of Daniel's building have daubed a slightly more detailed statement one street away. It explains to anyone willing to read it that spraying house fronts is a practical measure against the gentrification of the area, as people will be less interested in investing in a locality prone to wild tagging. This isn't always the correct conclusion, though: you can judge if a neighbourhood is up and coming by the quality of its street art.

Daniel has only recently settled here. In the preceding years he lived in Kreuzberg on the other side of the canal. He moved back from East Berlin in 1995 to Naunynstrasse in the punk and squat heartland of Kreuzberg. Several members of the notorious Kreuzberg gang 36 Boys lived in the same building as he did. Their name was derived from the old postcode SO 36, which is still used to distinguish the part of Kreuzberg with a higher migrant population from the old 61, traditionally home to academics.

'The people in the building were all fine. It was a cool place. I think I was the only German. It had only one disadvantage: there was a vacant plot opposite with a cockerel living there who'd always crow at two in the morning. Every time I'd decided to have an early night and was just falling asleep – cock-a-doodle-doo! Every single night.'

Kreuzberg didn't just look like a non-conformist village; there really were chickens roosting in some places. There were still many traces of the time when the district used to be a quiet spot on the easternmost edge of the Western world, populated by hippies, squatters, punks and anarchists, but home in particular to people recruited as guest workers after the war. In spite or perhaps because of this, tourism and the property market were playing an ever greater role in neighbourhood life. People from all over Europe bought flats for themselves – Scandinavians, the Brits and the French because real estate was cheap; Greeks and Italians because they wanted a safe place for their money. Entire buildings were converted into holiday apartments.

Daniel Pflumm still can't quite understand the debate that has obsessed the whole city in recent years. 'You could see it unfolding in Mitte over a span of ten years. The pace of it left you clutching your head in your hands – overnight, buildings would be lit up by spotlights and fitted with gold-plated door handles. And now here the rest of them are, ten years later, discovering gentrification. What's worst is that it's a crime with an invisible perpetrator.' The people complaining about this upgrading are often the same individuals who set the process in motion in their neighbourhood. 'They come here from Darmstadt and do their whole Darmstadt thing here. After a while, without their even noticing, their area looks just like Darmstadt. Then they cross the street and say, "It's awfully quiet here now"', Daniel says.

The influx of people from the provinces was a paradoxical process. A shortage of alternatives forced them to pursue their desire to see or experience something of life. Fed up of life in the sticks, they moved to the city, where they reinvented themselves as members of a band or as a DJ, writer, painter, graphic designer or gallerist. The clubs, bars and galleries of the nineties were also places where people from the backwaters came together with others who'd lived in a city all their life. Berliners themselves, cooped up until very recently, sometimes struck the people from the provinces as being very provincial. If you'd grown up in Lichtenrade or Lichtenberg, your own neighbourhood wasn't necessarily a particularly cosmopolitan place. And yet the Berlin mentality was that of a large city, maybe because many people here were the descendants of uprooted migrant workers from Silesia and elsewhere who washed up from the mid-nineteenth century onwards to work in the city's factories. Along with their villages they also abandoned their rural habits.

Berliners are definitely more quick-witted. Provinciality and urbanity depend to some extent on where you're from, but their expression in lifestyle and attitudes ultimately depends on a person's individual personality. There are absurd debates in Berlin nowadays over whether a Swabian living at Kollwitzplatz is too Swabian in his behaviour. The new conservatism that took hold in some parts of the city was also related to the newcomers' small-town narrow-mindedness. More than anything, though, it was an expression of people's fear of so much mobility and upheaval.

Daniel Pflumm was born in Geneva but grew up in Berlin. He spent a year in New York when he was twenty. One tell-tale indication that he isn't the provincial kind of Berliner is his attitude to tourism. He thinks that people who complain about gentrification should be happy about tourists because tourists are the first sign that a neighbourhood's value is on the wane.

'The main point, though, is that by the time you start asking questions about gentrification, you've already com-promised too much.'

It's a hot summer's day. Daniel is wearing white jeans, a short-sleeved, patterned shirt and espadrilles. This is the plain, modern style, the bohemian tendencies noticeable only in the details. Typical early nineties Mitte. Even now, partying foreign tourists find they're too well dressed for Berlin's clubs. Wearing trainers can be interpreted as a state-ment. Which it is, but that's not to say there aren't other reasons for doing so – no one can dance for eight hours in high heels.

Daniel says there are no places left to organize parties. First there was the Elektro, then the Panasonic. Later on, Daniel and his mates used the Init pop-up art gallery, run by Galerie Neu. In recent years Daniel has regularly invited people to DJ at his studio, but over time he got simply too much hassle from the property managers. It has become dif-ficult to find a studio cheap enough to hold events that don't need to make a profit. If rents are too high, the risk is that people fall into what Daniel refers to as the 'gastronomy trap'.

There's nothing gentrified about Daniel's flat. It looks more like a squat the occupants have fixed up for a temporary stay. The walls are still covered with the old wallpaper, which lends the rooms character. There's very little furniture other than a bed and a range of tables with equipment on them, surrounded by piles of documents and books. Postcards and photos have been stuck on the walls. Crumpled paper balls have accumulated in a small heap in one corner – a temporary home for finished business. Everything has its own place, nothing is superfluous.

Conceptual rigour and an eye for essentials are apparent not only in Daniel's video art but also in the design of the Elektro at Mauerstrasse 15, which was part of his artistic production. He made his name in the latter half of the 1990s as an artist who worked with Galerie Neu, and in the 2000s he enjoyed international success with his videos and lightboxes. His works focus on questions of communication, how it is organized, in what conditions and to what ends.

He manipulates the logos of international corporations, the conventions of TV news and the clean imagery of commercials. One of his best videos reduces the format of the TV interview to an absurd spectacle by looping a sequence of the interaction between two people on the CNN programme *Q & A* during a moment when they both happen to be silent. The host and the interviewee have stopped doing what they usually do, namely summing up the state of the world in a few precise statements. They are both staring silently at the camera. The only thing happening is the play of the emotions on their faces. Sometimes a muscle will twitch, occasionally one of them will blink. Communication grinds to a halt; the dreaded moment of silence in a conversation between two people goes on forever.

Daniel Pflumm combines sequences from TV ads where liquids are poured into bowls, soup splashes into more soup and dishwasher tabs dissolve in water with a fizz. He also superimposes international brand logos at such speed that they become virtually impossible to differentiate while still remaining oddly recognizable. Daniel appropriates logos and projects them inside his handmade lightboxes. Occasionally he removes a brand's lettering from the graphic frame of its logo, leaving shapes that seem only vaguely familiar because the essential message is missing.

He started to look more closely at logos in the early nineties. 'I was always interested in neon signs and logos', he says. 'Even on the cardboard boxes TV sets or similar products came in. Industry, whether it was Esso or Dr. Oetker, more or less controlled advertising back then. Industrial design was far more advanced than ad agencies, or more advanced than any in Berlin at least. Industrial graphics were the ultimate. Logos weren't a weak spot but a spot we knew absolutely nothing about – how good graphics influenced our behaviour. When you put the graphics to a different purpose . . .'

Daniel Pflumm doesn't finish his sentence, suggesting that everyone needs to draw their own conclusions. He's amazed that the consumers targeted by company logos don't even seem to be aware of what is being constantly thrust in front of their eyes.

'Back then, TV stations could do whatever they wanted', he says. 'When I exhibited my lightboxes around the world, people would ask, "Which logo's that?" If I hung up the Dr. Oetker logo in the Staatsgalerie in Stuttgart and a hundred people came and asked what the logo was, it means they haven't ever really taken notice of it. Or else that they did recognize it but couldn't tell which logo it was. The terrifying thing about that was that the logo was graphically so perfect. It gave the company free rein to influence people. We recognize logos subconsciously.'

Anyone slipping through the gap in the Wall near Checkpoint Charlie and stepping out into Friedrichstrasse after the Wende wasn't only leaving the American sector behind. Crossing the old zonal border into the East also meant escaping from the iconography of the West. The western part of the city was full of logos, pictures and neon signs, whereas the urban space in East Berlin was virtually devoid of imagery. Real existing socialism was byzantine not only in its bureaucratic control of every aspect of people's lives, but also in its aversion to visual production. After the collapse of the East German state, the logos came flooding in. Images of Western goods generated new desires and swamped the Wild East – a huge, untapped market.

Tobacco brands were the pioneers. The über-logo of the West cigarette brand, its very name synonymous with the world of Western consumption, was everywhere. The slogan of its inaugural campaign in the East was 'Test the West!' It stood out perfectly against the dull brown background of the buildings, its only rival in the first few months after the fall of the Wall being the occasional bright-green artificial grass strip, dotted with Monobloc plastic chairs, outside a snack bar or tobacco stand. Although Western TV stations beamed their messages into East Germany, the cities remained largely untouched by advertising. Soon, however, the neon logos of transnational electronics corporations began to blaze down on Alexanderplatz.

Now, in 1992, a small former shop at Mauerstrasse 15 is displaying lightboxes, one decorated with the white Panasonic logo against a blue background, the other the red and yellow logo of Elektro on a black background. Panasonic is a famous brand; Elektro is not.

The year 1990 marks the beginning of a trend in Mitte to adopt the name people find before they change the purpose of a premises: Elektro, Farben, Friseur, Obst & Gemüse or WMF. Adapting the existing description of the business is a form of understatement as well as a token of consideration for the space's previous occupant.

But Daniel Pflumm goes one step further. Along with the name, he also adopts the font he finds on the shopfront in Mauerstrasse, which he initially uses as a studio. Attached to the wall above the shop window, in uppercase letters, is the word 'Elektro', surrounded by a plain, sober rectangle. The typography is adapted from the one used by the West German industrial standards agency. It's an unspectacular font in keeping with modern design, and although it was probably not intended as a logo, it works perfectly as one.

The electrical goods store at Mauerstrasse 15 goes back a long time. After 1936, the premises to the right of the entrance were occupied by the Winkelmann electrical installation agency. It is apparent from a photo taken in 1950 that the name was changed either just before or just after the war: the business traded then as Wino. The goods it sold are advertised on the shopfront: light and power devices, lamps, motors and radios.

At some point between 1950 and 1983, an uncredited designer must have set to work and come up with the Elektro logo. In the summer of 1983 employees of the Mapping and Assessment Centre of the VEB Combine Geodesics and Cartography paid a visit to Mauerstrasse. One of the buildings they photographed and surveyed was number 15. A document was subsequently filed away in the records; it includes a black-and-white photograph on which the logo is clearly visible. The picture is annotated with the precise dimensions of the features on the facade, the front door, the windows and the distances between them. A closer look at these measurements reveals that the housefront has an anomaly that completely defines the overall look of the building but would not have come to light without the aid of the VEB Combine Geodesics and Cartography. The windows of the top two storeys are not vertically aligned with those on the three floors below. The upper windows are offset slightly to the right.

The existence of this document filed in 1983 triggered an amusing idea in Mo Loschelder's head thirty years later: you could replicate this building if you wanted to. Mo Loschelder organized parties at the Elektro and later ran the label Elektro Music Department jointly with Klaus Kotai and Daniel Pflumm. It would be genuinely possible to rebuild the house in Mauerstrasse. Architects also came and surveyed it after the Wende when it was being considered if the building ought to be listed or not.

It is clear from the VEB document that the original rounded arches over the shop window and the front door were walled up at some stage. There were curtains hanging in the windows in 1983, and it was obviously no longer in use as an electrical goods store. Sometime between 1983 and 1990, the sign above the shop window succumbed to the combined effects of gravity and the weather; the materials had worn away. By the time the Wall came down, the lower third of the E and part of the K in Elektro were missing.

Daniel Pflumm adapts the sign and reproduces it. 'It was virtually my first official act on a computer', he says, 'and it was also the first logo I designed on one.'

The first flyers Daniel designs – also on the computer – show the intact Elektro logo. A later reproduction is of the logo in its original state: Daniel has incorporated the damage to the letters E and K. This is a stroke of genius for two reasons: first, a damaged logo is even more seductive than a whole one because it conveys a sense of transience; second, it fills the Elektro logo with life and history. It stands for its past and its origins at Mauerstrasse 15; a particular place and a particular time combine to form a symbol.

For his adaptation of the grey relief letters on the wall Daniel uses the traditional colours of the electrical trade: red lettering and a red box on a yellow background.

He adds to the logo the slogan 'Full Customer Satisfaction', which he discovers on a plastic display unit he brings to the Elektro. This logo can be seen all over Berlin and elsewhere in the following years, printed on black and green T-shirts. At first the back of the T-shirt sports the words 'Full Customer Satisfaction', but Daniel soon alters this claim to 'Total Customer Satisfaction'. The wearer of an Elektro T-shirt is identifiably a Berlin subculture connoisseur.

'A particular type of young man wore UR and Elektro T-shirts', Mari Lippok says. UR is the logo of the Detroit techno collective Underground Resistance, who were much loved and celebrated in Berlin.

Initially, Daniel used the premises of the old electrical goods shop for his work, but he later lived there. One day he got to know the people in the WMF building next door.

'The nasty lads from the band Fleischmann! It was said in our building that there was bother with the Fleischmann guys. They'd allegedly chucked stones through someone's windows. I went over to WMF with a posse from our building to set things straight. We got to the top where the nasty Fleischmann lads lived and were greeted by Tom and Gerriet. They were very understanding. They hadn't done it, of course – they really didn't have time for smashing windows. It was the first time I ever dozed off during a fight', Daniel recalls.

There was room in the WMF building and so he moved in, freeing up his studio. The old shop now became the Elektro.

At first the Elektro was a shop with a bar that sold oddball products. Daniel got Juri, Bym and Clé, DJ friends of his from WMF, to record DJ mixtapes.

'We opened with four tapes, but by the end there were about ten. We played the tapes in the shop. We had a stereo from the beginning – a hi-fi which was very quiet. It was planned as a shop selling DJ mixtapes, art on floppy disks, jackets, caps and T-shirts.'

You had to go up three steps into the shop. Three more steps led from the lower room with the shop window into a second one where Daniel and his mates built a small metal-clad bar. This was where beer was served and the cassette deck operated. Later on, the counter also accommodated two Technics turntables and a mixing console.

To free up the view from the bar into the lower room, Daniel Pflumm and Raquel Eulate asked two demolition experts from the WMF building to knock a hole in the wall. Now you could look through from the top room to the bottom room. The products of Haus Elektro were displayed on a shelf behind the bar. The mixtapes' yellow covers were stamped with the red Elektro logo and the relevant DJs' names. Daniel put a wheeled clothes rack in the lower room and hung on it T-shirts and bomber jackets, made by Johanna Myhrberg, which he'd emblazoned with the Microsoft, Panasonic and Elektro logos. Artisanal tailoring and ripped-off logos created a fashionable symbiosis. The range also included a red woollen beanie with the Microsoft logo on it. The minimalist, modernist style of the Elektro and its products was the brightly coloured antithesis of the melancholic junk aesthetic of the squatters in the Spandauer Vorstadt.

'Daniel was the most independent of us all. He always managed to do exactly what he wanted. He didn't care what anybody thought, and that was why the Elektro was unlike anywhere else. Those places always reflect the personality of the people who created them', Raquel Eulate says.

Daniel has an even simpler explanation for what occurred at the Elektro. 'It was the end of the eighties, which were so grim that you really didn't have to do much to have a good time. A bit like now.'

In bed with Mo

Daniel Pflumm heard a woman DJing in the tiled rooms of a former Invalidenstrasse butcher's shop now known as Mutzek. He asked her for a mixtape for his shop and got one.

Mo Loschelder moved to Berlin in the winter of 1990 while following the Californian hardcore punk band Saccharine Trust around Germany. She had studied art under Gerhard Richter in Düsseldorf and was considering going to London or Amsterdam to add on a Master's.

'That was the plan, but then I came to Berlin and I knew I had to stay because it was far too exciting to go anywhere else.'

Mo lived in Kreuzberg first, then two weeks later she discovered Tacheles. She moved into a squat in Auguststrasse before living for a while in a studio Jutta Weitz arranged for her. The two women first bumped into each other at a tram stop in Oranienburger Strasse.

'I was at Tacheles one night. It was really late and there was no tram in sight', Jutta remembers. 'There was a couple standing next to me and we started chatting. It was Mo Loschelder and her fellow painter Lukas Duwenhoegger. They were annoyed that the tram was late because they were planning to go to the housing association the next morning and apply for a space. They'd heard that there was this woman who might be able to help them. I didn't say anything. The trams had stopped for the night, Mo and Lukas had to go to Prenzlauer Berg, I was going to Prenzlauer Berg and so we set off on foot together. When we got to Senefelder Platz where I was living, I invited them up for a cup of tea. My name wasn't marked on the door, only my boyfriend's, so there was no chance they'd get suspicious.'

The very next morning Mo Loschelder stood in front of Jutta's desk, eyes wide with amazement. Decades later, she still has warm memories of the circumstances of their meeting.

Mo used to go to Ständige Vertretung in the basement of Tacheles to dance, often staying until closing time and then moving on with the barkeepers to the Tresor.

'It would be rocking there in the early hours. After the first two steps, you couldn't see anything on your way down into the cellar. You'd be in this thick fog. We often went to the Bunker or some basement club that was only open for a few weeks.'

Mo's clubbing in Mitte had consequences. Within a year, she went from being a painter to performing as a DJ called Mobody, later shortened to Mo. At first, her sets were a wild mix of genres including soul, hip-hop, Indian music and French chansons because she tried to play as much music by women as possible – a principle that precluded any notion of stylistic unity. Mo generally didn't fade tracks in. 'Not mixing is an attitude, not negligence', she told a *taz* reporter. She was playing such a variety of records at the time that there was no point in mixing them.

One of her first performances was part of a project Mo organized with some female friends at the Galerie Art Acker. People were puzzled by its provocative title: 'Women Try to Play Records.' Much to Mo's pleasure, this proved beyond most arty types' capacity for irony. Yet she was more serious than today's post-feminist mainstream about tackling the issue of why there are so few women DJs and record producers. Nowadays she looks back with amazement at how many female DJs played at the Friseur, the Elektro and elsewhere. And it wasn't only behind the mixing console that women were active – in Mitte it was often women who ran the show. The men built houses and clubs; through their work for local authorities, housing associations, clubs and bars, women put in place the structures underpinning the new culture of Mitte.

Why women? 'Because men weren't interested in doing a lot of work for little glory', is the theory Dolly Leupold came up with from her work at Mitte council's cultural department. However, lots of women wanting to DJ was also a sign that they were no longer content to toil away in the shadows.

'It's not like that nowadays, and it's an issue I often face as an agent', says Mo, who now runs a booking agency. Sitting in the Prenzlauer Berg flat she shares with her husband and daughter, she flicks through her flyer collection to retrace the early years of her career as a DJ and holds one up. 'This was the first party where I was booed and heckled. A lesbian party at Subversiv.'

Berlin's lesbian community was well known for its conservative music tastes. Old photos show how androgynous Mo looked at the time; with her short hair and baggy T-shirts, she was occasionally mistaken for a man. In one picture she is standing in front of a housing block in Mitte in white hot-pants, blue platform sandals and a dark-blue T-shirt.

Mo's first fans were Kai and Olof. The two of them had grown up in Prenzlauer Berg, had just turned twenty and lived in a place in Dunckerstrasse. They ran a mini-club called Dauerwelle [Perm] in an old shop a few buildings away, and would regularly invite Mo to DJ there.

'Dauerwelle looked a bit as if Schinkel had designed it', she says. 'It was a small, almost square room painted royal blue. The stucco moulding along the edges of the ceiling was gilded, and in the middle there was this glitterball hanging down, which created a night-sky effect. There was only room for the DJ, and the bar and the cloakroom were next door.'

Kai and Olof went to great pains to put on spectacular parties like 'In Bed with Mo' – a tongue-in-cheek allusion to the documentary film *In Bed with Madonna*, and at the same time a literal description.

'It was my idea. I dreamed up the title. The lads got hold of the beds – discarded hospital beds. I brought along the sheets and pillows. All the partygoers came with their pyjamas, and they got breakfast in bed the next morning', Mo says.

The very first techno record she played at Dauerwelle was 'Rings of Saturn' by X-102, a moniker used by Jeff Mills, Mike Banks and Robert Hood from Detroit. Mo mixed the album with the soundtrack of the 1960s West German science-fiction series *Raumpatrouille Orion* [*Space Patrol Orion*].

'It worked great because of the futuristic side to the two records', she says.

Some people were catapulted into a different orbit by being thrown out of East Germany or the fall of the Wall, but in Mo's case it was the clubs of Mitte and working the turntables. After DJing a few times, she lost all interest in galleries. Whereas she would have once spent the whole day painting, now she devoted herself to music. She produced one last two-picture series, each featuring an exotic, topless pin-up girl. Mo took a photo of the motif on TV and then transposed it to canvas. What her paintings and her music had in common, she says, is that they had no narrative.

The new music created space for people to move. That was appropriate for Mitte, where there were two kinds of space – empty buildings, and a temporary haziness around social space. The reason house and techno were able to grow within a few years into a mass movement was because anyone and everyone could identify with this music.

Fig. 12 Mo Loschelder and Julian Göthe DJing

The radical difference between her old life as an artist and her new one as a DJ was that Mo Loschelder no longer worked alone.

'Before, I used to stand in my studio on my own. I enjoyed that too. There's the same impulse in music to change the world through your own personal intervention. My real realization, though, was that music is a language for shared experience. I discovered what it means to do things that only come about because there are other people there with you, whether you're listening or dancing, DJing alongside someone or making music together. I was very conscious of the new direction I was taking, and that's also why I stopped painting because I wanted to experience it with that intensity. It defined the course of my life.'

She was not alone. Mo Loschelder's transformation as an artist was mirrored at a larger scale. Painting faded into the background; art was once again about concepts. Institutionalized museums and galleries were subjected to criticism. Works of art were no longer produced for the 'white cube' – the gallery's empty space – but placed in a relation with the places where they were created. DJs were elevated to prominent artistic figures, and no preview was complete without one. Clubs appeared to be more productive places than galleries. For a short space of time, the new music was the medium that could channel all the energy released by the upheaval and direct it towards the future – a word that sounded positive again after the apocalyptic atmosphere of the eighties. The traditional narrative forms of song and album were replaced by tracks. You could listen to these at home of course, but they only achieved their full effect when DJs combined them with other tracks. What mattered was not *whether* a specific track was played, but *when* it was played. Ideally, the DJs created a musical arc that took the dancers on a night-long journey together. What counted was the intensity of the moment everyone shared. Mo had to learn to mix.

Anti-money-grabbing

Soon after Mo Loschelder handed Daniel Pflumm her first mixtape at the Elektro, they threw a party together. It was such a success that the next one soon followed, and quickly the concept bar with the tapes and T-shirts developed into a club where international stars like Robert Hood and Dave

Clarke manned the decks. They would drop in before or after stints at big local clubs. They liked the Elektro because they could play whatever they liked there. The Elektro's programme increasingly revolved around house and techno because Mo started working at Hard Wax record shop and her colleague Electric Indigo had good connections within the scene. Techno grandmaster Jeff Mills announced several times that he'd come and DJ and one time his name even featured on one of the Elektro's yellow-and-red flyers, but when the day came, he didn't show up.

Who did turn up one evening, though, were Khan & Walker, hooking up their decks on the counter because there was no room anywhere else.

'We never played for less than six hours, and we did the same there. People passed beers over our mixing console, and drinks got inside the drum machine. Everyone was there, every pioneering DJ and producer in Berlin, and they all lost their sense of time and space. The next morning, we were let out into a foggy, grey, empty city and we were happy', Can Oral, aka Khan, remembers.

On 10 April 1994 he and his partner Walker performed at the Elektro, as is apparent from the label of the red vinyl record they had pressed soon afterwards. It contains four of the night's highpoints. A few weeks after their appearance, one of them dropped in at the Elektro with the discs, which boasted 'Live at the Electro', complete with spelling mistake.

Just because techno now ruled the Elektro didn't mean that no other music was played. Stefan Schulz, alias Nucleus, and Tilmann soon set up shop at the Elektro too and played their own programme, which also had room for funk, disco and house.

'There were two camps at the Elektro. I was between the two, I listened to everything – I didn't mind. They all did amazing things the whole time', Daniel Pflumm says.

Stefan Schulz and Tilmann got Bass Dee and Feed to perform at the Elektro. Bass Dee was eighteen, Feed fifteen. They turned up from Zehlendorf in their parents' Mercedes and were soon DJing regularly at the club. For a while Mondays were hip-hop night, which meant that kids tagged all the walls and speakers. Sometimes sprayers would burst through the door, scrawl their names on a wall and head out again. Soon the Elektro looked like a cross between an underground station and a New Wave bar, more in keeping with one of William Gibson's cyberpunk novels than the real-life city centre of Berlin.

One night the deaf activist Gunter Trube celebrated his birthday at the Elektro with his mates. Standing on the counter in a fifties apron like some post-war West Berlin drag queen, he reeled off a stream of obscene anecdotes. Gunter Trube was a virtuoso signer, so even people who didn't understand sign language caught his gist. This was followed by dancing – the basses had to be turned up extra loud. Mo Loschelder remembers that the deaf particularly loved records by the Berlin-based techno producer Basic Channel because their basslines were well modulated. But one man's full-body massage was a breach of the peace to a sleeping neighbour. The police frequently came calling at the Elektro.

'I heard that the police came once to find the music on full blast but no one behind the bar. People were just sitting around. Eventually the police turned down the sound themselves and asked if anyone spoke German. They did, but no one wanted to own up to being the boss. Once there was a shitty nappy hanging from the door handle with a note saying we'd woken the kids up again, so we were a bit quieter for a week', Daniel Pflumm says.

Mo is responsible for interacting with the authorities. 'I took care of that kind of thing. I had to write a letter

Fig. 13 Party at the Elektro, with Jeff Mills and Electric Indigo in the crowd

expressing our dismay at mistreating the working population. We always got off lightly.'

The Elektro's biggest ever party was during the 1994 Love
Parade. That summer Slavko Stefanoski played his part in
what he calls the 'daily science fiction of Mauerstrasse'. He set
up a garden between Mauerstrasse 15 and the WMF building.

'There was a vacant plot next to the Mauerhaus and on it
was this small building – supposedly the Finnish embassy's
sauna. It had caught fire in spring 1994, the hut was gutted
and the doors were wide open. I had to do some real spade-
work to turn my vision into reality. There was a pond with
floating candles and a little tree in the corner. There was a
table and four chairs, and I had a huge armchair. I made it
look pretty, you could say, and then anyone was welcome to
use it for whatever he or she wanted. It worked brilliantly,
everyone came, even the neighbours from the blocks opposite, and I served them tea and cake.'

During the Love Parade, two Brits parked their van in Slavko's garden and cooked a big tub of soup which they shared around when the parade poured into the city centre. 'The Love Parade was a dream. People were sitting around in the streets like flowers. It was a culture, a dream of a better world – through internet, through peace and also sex. That might sound stupid, but it was a movement, a way of looking at the world. We were living in the centre of the world', Slavko says.

The 1994 Love Parade was held on 2 July. One hundred and twenty thousand ravers flooded along the Kurfürstendamm. Techno had grown into a movement and gatecrashed the charts. Marusha sang 'Somewhere Over the Rainbow', and Camel and Puma were the parade's main sponsors.

'Techno is now used as a soundtrack to sell rucksacks to schoolchildren, make a stand against the decimation of whales or start a family', Harald Fricke, the incorruptible chronicler of Mitte culture, had written a year earlier.

The parade took place on a Saturday afternoon and the partying went on until Monday morning. Some forty lorries carried sound systems through the City West area, and among them was the Elektro's van.

'We organized our own vehicle and shared it with DJ Hell, who came up with the idea', Daniel Pflumm says. 'The others, Stefan and Tilmann, kept going, "Oh no, oh no!" I didn't think it was such a bad idea – imagine the Elektro at the Love Parade on a hire van from Robben & Wientjes.'

It was the kind of small van typically used for moving house, but at the Love Parade it was a statement. The Elektro's sound system was the smallest in the parade. The vehicle's suspension was terrible and so the turntable needle kept jumping, though this didn't seem to bother the Elektro van's retinue as the team showered the following crowd with water from pump guns. Unlike the techno labels and other clubs, most of which could only cover the participation fee through sponsorship deals, the Elektromobile rolled through the city free of charge.

'DJ Hell got us a bargain', Daniel says. 'Other people would definitely have fancied doing the same thing – it would've been fantastic if loads of car-boot ravers could've brought their cars to the parade.'

The producers of the like-minded Finnish label Säkhö (meaning 'electricity') were doing a guest set at the Elektro. Taking inspiration from the lightbox there, they changed their name to Panasonic soon afterwards. This triggered a lawsuit from the electronics firm and, banned from calling themselves Panasonic, they subsequently morphed into Pan Sonic.

There were always people sleeping on the open space between the Friseur and the Elektro, during the Love Parade, no matter what the time was. The Elektro stayed open around the clock all weekend, and Daniel got so exhausted that he toppled over behind the counter.

'I thought I'd better go home. I woke up again at half past twelve on Monday wondering if it was day or night, and if the party had already finished. It was the day Dave Clarke was DJing for us, so I got over to the Elektro fast.'

By the time he reached the Elektro, Mauerstrasse was packed with ravers.

'Sven Väth was enthroned on a chair someone had attached to an old, rectangular East German coat stand, and was sitting outside the Elektro, rambling on about something or other. I went up to him and said, "Tell everybody to pipe down or there's going to be trouble." He told them. The 1994 Love Parade was the best Love Parade ever. Kids from out in Brandenburg were roaming the city, looking for a party. They had rubber boots on and spiky hairstyles. Adults didn't get it. It was its own bubble – basically, punk

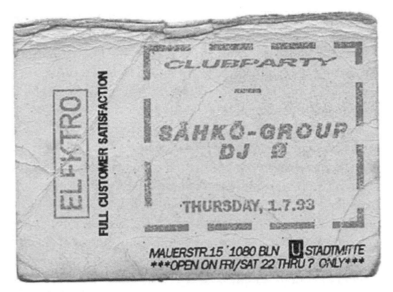

Fig. 14 An Elektro flyer announcing the Säkhö Group

by other means. A movement with its own codes. If you hear some music no one understands, then someone else likes it and you get together, then it's like encryption. Techno was a conspiratorial movement against pop stars and the cult of celebrity. There were rules based on a consensus, and then there were counter-revolutionaries like Sven Räth. The last time we were in touch was when I sent him a bill for the twenty vodkas he'd ordered and was served at the Elektro on the Monday morning of the Love Parade.'

On that first July weekend in 1994 the entire city centre was full of ravers and music. Clusters of people had set up camps everywhere, and every vacant site was occupied.

'And nothing came of it! On the other hand, the fact that the Love Parade went the way it did might be a fittingly tragic ending for a myth. Right to the end it was a political demonstration, that was hijacked not only by the people who milked it commercially but also by the Senate, which kept setting new requirements', Daniel says.

Initially, the authorities wanted to deny the 1994 Love Parade the status of demonstration. If Thomas Krüger, who was now senator for youth, hadn't thrown his weight behind the parade, it would probably have been cancelled.

Raquel Eulate was working at the Elektro that Love Parade weekend – her final shift before moving to London. She cut herself on the sharp edge of the old fridge behind the bar. 'It wouldn't stop bleeding, but I couldn't leave – it was too full. I still have the scar to remind me of the Elektro.'

There was a monitor mounted on the wall in one corner of the lower room. It screened videos, for example *Hallo TV*.

'Originally, I went out and asked people to say hallo to my camera', Daniel Pflumm says.

Daniel made *Hallo TV* by editing a compilation of people saying hallo, either outside the Elektro or elsewhere, and the series just grew and grew. You never heard the word 'Hallo' in the Elektro, though, because the sound was turned off and the background music was loud. Daniel later collaborated with Gereon Schmitz to expand the idea of *Hallo TV*.

'We always wanted to get on television, but it never panned out that way. We were so desperate to get on TV that we even went to see Panasonic and their advertising agency. We had an idea we called "Nightline", an ambient night-time programme we would make for any station that wanted it. Panasonic was supposed to finance it. Our plan was to travel all over the world, filming motorway trips and train and underground journeys at night. We took the Berlin underground and drove on the city expressway and went up the television tower. We wanted to make a series about revolving cafés worldwide. *Hallo TV* kept broadcasting throughout and still does, despite Gereon no longer being with us. I'm pretty sure he's still a roving reporter for *Hallo TV* somewhere, and so am I', Daniel concludes.

The footage of the underground trains and the view from Berlin's television tower would be shown on the screen in the Elektro, and the footage also featured in Daniel Pflumm's later video art and the clips for the tracks by Kotai + Mo that came out on the Elektro Music Department label after its original namesake ceased to exist.

Mo Loschelder met Klaus Kotai in Munich and started making her own music with him. Kotai + Mo's analogue electronic sound is minimalistic, dark and warm, reminiscent of the music of the electropunk band Deutsch Amerikanische Freundschaft. Voices can be heard over simple basslines, but at times they are so distorted by filters, effects and cut-ups that you can't understand them, and sometimes the desire to lose oneself in the other comes across loud and clear: 'There's a gift waiting in the morning for you.'

Elektro was not a place of entertainment; Elektro was the corporate identity of a work of art, created with the help of many hands as a permanent source of new ideas, parties, conversations and encounters. Sometimes there were only a handful of people to listen to the trance jazz of a DJ called Der Lächelnde Schamane – the Smiling Shaman. Stefan Schulz can remember many quiet nights.

'The Elektro was empty at first. Many nights, there were just the two of us. The door would open ten times, people would peer inside . . . and then leave again. It took a year for the Elektro to establish itself.'

When Jim Lusted, who was responsible for one of those mixtapes, organized British band the Stereo MCs' after-show party at the Elektro, only ten people came. That flop still tickles Daniel Pflumm and Mo Loschelder now: Mo was worried it would get too full and told her friends to keep it totally secret, while Daniel forgot to distribute the flyers.

'The Elektro was the most radical space in Mitte. Open a place like that and you come under immediate pressure to fill it. No one at the Elektro cared how popular the place was', Raquel Eulate says.

It only worked because Mauerstrasse 15 was a squat.

'If you don't have to pay any rent, you can afford the luxury of not charging an entrance fee. I thought it was great we could avoid things like a door policy. It was anti-money-grabbing. The same at the Friseur. It also distinguished us from the other clubs nearby like the Tresor, E-Werk and all the rest of them. Whether they were actually able to make any money is a different matter, but their proprietors must have looked out for themselves financially. We never ever dreamed of an Elektro Tower, anyway', Mo Loschelder says, alluding to Tresor club boss Dimitri Hegemann's megalomaniac dream of a 'Tresor Tower' overlooking Potsdamer Platz.

'We took that liberty', Daniel Pflumm adds. 'That was the whole point – to occupy a place where people could meet. That's the only reason there's a club scene in Berlin. The whole thing developed because we were able to experiment while the spaces were still cheap. Nowadays, whatever they're doing, people try to make as much money as possible. That isn't necessarily positive for society, but the system basically forces you to act that way. No one breaks their back for fun.'

The Elektro was shut down by the police in December 1994. Handshake, a group of media and internet artists, had set up a Clubnetz terminal in the bar that allowed people there to chat with clubbers elsewhere via Internet Relay Chat. However, because Mauerstrasse 15 wasn't connected to the phone network, they used to hook the terminal up to the line of the supermarket next door at the weekend. One Sunday evening, though, when Clubnetz was usually switched off again, they shut down the supermarket's connection by mistake.

'That night, we suddenly had the police searching the premises, shining their torches everywhere and saying, "We're here because you're using a phone line illegally. We can see you've been tapping electricity illegally too." And then they told us to turn everything off and get out. And so we did', Mo says.

One year later, Daniel Pflumm, Mo Loschelder and Klaus Kotai opened the Panasonic in Mutzek's old place in Invalidenstrasse. After two years they moved to the Init art hall, which was run by Galerie Neu in an old supermarket just around the corner in Chausseestrasse. For some time afterwards, the Elektro Music Department label carried on releasing music by Kotai + Mo, Daniel Pflumm and guests. Daniel threw parties at his studio and put his artistic career on hold. He set up two more labels and produced records for a range of different formations. Mo Loschelder started painting again.

'People tend to underestimate how much a project like the Elektro relies on a particular constellation of people, and that as soon as certain people leave, the whole thing stops functioning. Habits play their part in how people interact with one another, who starts the engine and pulls the others along. If that no longer works, then that chapter is closed', Mo says.

The spirit of the Elektro is still alive and well, sustained by the sprawling network of websites Daniel Pflumm has sown online. It's easy to get lost following the links hidden behind blinking logos, design elements and slogans, the abiding impression being of a myriad of planets orbiting a black hole. The hall of mirrors created by the allusions, bright logos, links and references stir up the beholder's own memories. Daniel's farewell message to visitors to his online interface is: 'The world is empty without you. Go out, prove your existence, live a life and cut this crap.'

5

The Nineteenth-Century 'Founders' of Berlin

The bulldozer moves in

'Those windows on the second floor, where you can see the glow of the monitors . . . That's Willi Pieck's study.' Jörg von Stein points out of his window overlooking Mauerstrasse at the building opposite. Wilhelm Pieck was the first president of the German Democratic Republic. His office is now occupied by a member of staff at the Federal Ministry of Labour and Social Affairs, which is led by Ursula von der Leyen.[1]

The building's first and most prominent resident was Dr Joseph Goebbels, Reichsminister for Public Enlightenment and Propaganda.

'Along with the Reichsbank, it was the first thing the Nazis built, but it wasn't designed by Speer or Sagebiel',[2]

---

[1] Ursula von der Leyen is now president of the European Commission.
[2] Ernst Sagebiel (1892–1970) was a German architect who rose to prominence in the Nazi era.

Jörg von Stein says. 'There was a block of baroque buildings here before, some of them one-storeyed. Their owners were expropriated, and an extra wing was added to the propaganda ministry.'

The main building of Goebbels's ministry was on the other, western side of the block on Wilhelmplatz. Goebbels had installed his offices in Prince Karl's former palace in 1933 in order to be constantly close to his Führer, as both the old and new Reich Chancellery were opposite his ministerial headquarters.

To get from his kitchen to his bathroom, Jörg has to cross the entire length of his apartment, through rooms painted in a variety of colours, each space communicating with the next. The building served as a brothel during the global economic crisis that followed the First World War, an activity to which the building's baroque floor plan was eminently well suited, as each room could be accessed directly from the staircase.

'Friedrichstrasse was an entertainment district in the late nineteenth and early twentieth centuries – pleasure gardens, as they were called at the time', Jörg explains. His grandmother told him how she used to watch attractive women strolling in the neighbouring streets during the twenties. It was from them that she learned to put on make-up properly and also how they earned their living. 'My grandmother was a genteel woman, but also a practical person. She told me that those women's job was to be nice to men.'

It is quite possible that the good-looking women in Friedrichstrasse sometimes took their customers to Wanda Klopp's hotel and guest house at Mauerstrasse 15, which had once marked the outer limit of the city's expansion in 1698, on the edge of old Friedrichstadt.

'That's why the street is built on a curve, because they were planning to erect another city wall. They didn't get

round to it, though, because that form of defence had actually become obsolete by the end of the seventeenth century',
Jörg says. Mauerstrasse was the narrowest and poorest street
in Friedrichstadt. 'It was where widows came to live. Women
would always live in the nicer parts of Friedrichstadt while
they were married and their situation was secure. But when
they were widowed and left without an inheritance, they'd
rent a few rooms in Mauerstrasse. They would take as many
rooms as they could afford and share a kitchen.'

The way people in Mauerstrasse got by after the fall of
the Wall is reminiscent of how they lived before the onset of
bourgeois society.

Jörg von Stein sprinkles his anecdotes about the neighbourhood between Friedrichstrasse and Wilhelmstrasse with
the occasional English word, which he pronounces with a
British accent. His father is from Berlin, but he himself grew
up in England.

'There can't be a more German-sounding name than Jörg
Heinrich Peter Freiherr von Stein, especially for someone
who grew up outside Germany, but it was only when I moved
to Berlin that I began to grasp the essence of Germanness,
this Prussian dimension. You notice what it means to be
Prussian here – both the positive and negative sides. There
are the old ladies who'll jam their stick in your spokes if you
cycle on the pavement, even for a few metres. Everyone in
Berlin is a self-appointed policeman, even now. It's really
odd.'

Jörg has lived in Mauerstrasse since the late nineties.
'There were more vacant properties in the old neighbourhoods in the East after the Wende than before. It caused
political outrage at the time', he says.

The Senate responded to this with a repair and lease
scheme by which tenants were required to renovate apartments in exchange for reduced rent. Everyone was desperate

to move to Mitte, but no one wanted to come to this area. Part of Jörg's flat was on the list, but not the rest because it was considered liable to collapse. The renovation work took two years.

'We rewired it, but it was no use because the mains system dated back to 1927. You had to choose between boiling water, vacuuming or running the washing machine.'

The building was partially 'Aryanized' by the Nazis. In 1934 the Reemtsma company purchased the whole block. The building was then fought over after the Wende, and, against all odds, ownership was granted to Berlin regional council. Despite the existence of a sociological study on the development of the government district, which came to the conclusion that it should be used for affordable housing, the regional council flogged the buildings at the first opportunity. The new owners dispatched heavies to von Stein's building to intimidate the tenants before they'd even acquired the building; Jörg successfully sued them.

Yet very few local tenants have shown Jörg's determination, and the results can still be seen around the corner in Taubenstrasse. Some windows are nailed up with particle board, and the facades still exhibit the same grey-brown hue that practically all buildings in Mitte displayed after the Wende.

'All of these houses used to be inhabited', Jörg recalls. 'Every single one of them has been sold on twenty times or more since then.'

The new owners didn't maintain the buildings, and sooner or later the exasperated tenants moved out of their own accord. Some of the houses have been unoccupied for years.

'Everything here is listed, and the owners are banking on the buildings collapsing. All of them have a baroque core, and if they remain empty for another ten years, it'll all go to ruin', he says.

Having worked for twelve years for a Berlin architectural agency specializing in the conservation of heritage assets, he knows a thing or two about baroque structures. It infuriates him that neither the Senate nor the district council are doing anything to combat the illegal practice of leaving properties vacant.

Jörg von Stein lives here in part because of the struggle against the demolition of Mauerstrasse 15.

'There was a Senate debate, and we were invited along as contact architects. When Mauerstrasse 15 came under threat of demolition, the debate was sabotaged by a group of people in extremely dramatic, but also highly amusing fashion.' A delegation from the Botschaft protested against the destruction. 'That was what first drew my attention to the area', he says. The building he now lives in is virtually identical to number 15.

In 1994 the *taz* published a list of 190 buildings threatened with demolition. In some cases, the concern was unfounded, in many only the facades could be saved, and a few were torn down.

Mauerstrasse 15 was on the list, and its big day came in December 1994. The building's owners demanded that the squatters move out within forty-eight hours, and soon it was empty. Number 15 and the courtyard building at Kronenstrasse 3 were to be replaced by a diplomatic centre at an estimated cost of seventy million marks – a welcome investment in a notoriously cash-strapped city. However, Mitte's councillor for construction, Dorothee Dubrau, an elected representative of Bündnis 90, campaigned for the building to be left standing. An expert report commissioned by the Magistrat before its demise concluded that this was the last building of its kind in the centre of Berlin. Conservation specialists believed that the bottom three floors dated back to around 1750, with the two upper floors added at a later date. In March 1995 it was placed under 'provisional protection', which meant that it couldn't be torn down in the next six months.

It was at this point, however, that Mauerstrasse became a political hot potato. Gerhard Keil, Mitte's SPD district mayor, relieved councillor Dubrau of responsibility for urban planning, heritage conservation and construction, accusing her of being hostile to investors. Her disempowerment triggered protests among other district councillors responsible for construction matters. On the other side of the political divide, the CDU welcomed the decision, saying that the centre of Berlin, the future seat of national government, could not afford to be held hostage by the Greens. The interests of investors were more important than a run-down baroque structure.

It was initially agreed that the building should be listed, but in the early hours of the very morning that the building was due to be placed on the list of heritage assets, the agreement was superseded by facts on the ground.

'The Senate knew when the bulldozers were going to come, but they sat on their hands', Jörg von Stein says.

It's a warm July night, the night between Tuesday and Wednesday, almost exactly a year after the great Love Parade party at the Elektro. Everything is following its usual course at the Friseur, where gin and tonics and bottles of beer are passed across the bar and DJs are spinning the decks. Then there's an earthquake-like shock to the sound, and someone goes to the door to see what's going on.

'They were out there with bulldozers, flattening Mauerstrasse 15', says Anton Waldt, who is on yet another night out in Kronenstrasse. The Friseur is like his living room. Outside, there is dust everywhere. 'They'd stuck notes on all the cars around the whole block. Their owners could go and pick up money for the car wash. They poked around at the building until a third of it caved in, then they stopped. The whole point, apparently, was to turn it into such a ruin that it could no longer be salvaged.'

When the workers and the bulldozers leave again, Anton Waldt and a few of his mates climb into the Elektro's bar room, which has been left unscathed.

'We could say our farewells. The folk from the Elektro hadn't cleaned up before they handed the place over. There were glasses and straws still lying around, so everyone picked a souvenir.'

Three days later, Anton Waldt is up on stage at the Friseur. The party has been planned a long time in advance, but now it turns into a requiem for the Elektro. Krautok begins on Friday 14 July 1995 and ends twenty-four hours later. It was only a matter of time before someone came up with the idea of extending a party into a full day's celebration. To push back the limits even further and conquer fresh territory. To find out if music can keep the human machine running non-stop. The idea is in the air, and the nineties wouldn't be the nineties if – no sooner said than done! – it isn't immediately put into practice.

'The driving force behind Krautok was pretty simple, really. All of us would sit around in the studio, producing like crazy', Anton Waldt says. 'The idea was that we might just as well do that on stage. Six or seven of us simply built a slightly larger live set. That was a pretty infectious idea at the time: the beat never stops.'

The Friseur is the obvious place to put on such an event because Anton Waldt and his mates constantly hang out there. 'We combined two things that had been part of the plan all along anyway, then we saw it through remorselessly – keep the thing simmering for twenty-four hours. It was a normal night at the Friseur – it just went on for even longer than usual', Anton says.

Krautok is organized by Toktok, whose name was ono-
matopoeically inspired by the beat of the bass drum. 'Toktok
was originally a band collective', Anton says. 'There were
ten of them when they first get together in 1994, but the
group gradually shrank. At Krautok there were Nerk, Fabian
Feyerabendt, C14 and me, but Robotnik were also at Krautok
with us. Andrea and Andreas Robotnik.'

The party starts at four on the Friday afternoon. As the
evening proceeds, it fills up with people dancing and cele-
brating before dying down again.

'That used to be a great time to sit outside the Friseur.
By morning, the audience had always gone home, but there
was this tenacious posse around Kriton and Tilmann, and
so we'd often hang around there until midday. We'd put a
sofa outside the door, a speaker in the window, and someone
would carry on DJing inside', Anton says.

At Krautok too, anyone left sits outside the next morning, while one lonely person works the drum machines and
sequencers inside.

'If in doubt, do nothing, just let the machines keep turning. But then people would start turning up again in the
early afternoon.' Anton can't remember how and when the
party ends and why it is never repeated.

A year after Krautok, Anton moved to Vienna for a few
years, and C14 dropped out to become a programmer. Their
Robotnik colleague Andrea went back to Swabia soon after
to take over the family firm, which produced special screws.
Everyone's sojourn in the cultural cosmos of Mitte was
temporary; at some stage life had to go on. The collective
projects collapsed in time to the city's return to normal.

'In 1995, 1996, the party was over in Mitte. It was the end
of a special era', Christoph Keller says. 'Lots of people on
both sides of town had dropped out of uni. They'd gone with

the flow and taken time out from normal life. Some of them couldn't get back in the saddle and just vanished because they didn't have enough money or any qualifications. It wasn't all about partying; it was existential too.'

By the second Krautok in 2006, eleven years after the seminal event, Anton Waldt had long since left the techno collective and was editor-in-chief of *De:Bug*. The 'magazine for electronic lifestyles', according to its strapline, was founded as part of the movement around the Friseur and WMF, another example of the scene's consolidation.

Sitting in Wedding at the table of his new-build flat, where all the internal walls have been removed in homage to the knock-throughs in Mitte, Anton Waldt doesn't seem to have changed much from the old pictures of him outside the Friseur. He is tall and slim, his hair is cropped short and he smokes. The young man in those old photos – the man Anton Waldt once was – is merely a little thinner in the face.

He was in his early twenties when he arrived in Berlin in May 1990. 'Of course, you can have the feeling at that age that you're having the time of your life almost anywhere, but it was definitely special to have a whole city as your playground. That doesn't happen everywhere. I suspect we'd have soon got bored of the established, rotting, stagnant Kreuzberg vibe if the Wall hadn't come down', he says.

But then, just after the Tresor opened its doors, he discovered the city centre.

'We, this group of kids who'd grown up with hardcore punk, stumbled down the stairs one evening into the cellar of the Tresor. It was rough enough for us.' Someone raised on punk needed very little encouragement to enjoy the new sound of Mitte. 'For two years we went to the Tresor just about every weekend. We listened to Marusha's bonkers programme and her atrociously amazing presenting style, but she did play some good music. Then we'd go to the

Tresor, come out again around six in the morning usually and then cycle home to Friedrichshain.'

Anton Waldt celebrated this twenty-four-hour party lifestyle in his influential columns, which appeared in various fanzines between 1998 and 2006; a compilation was published later as a book. No one has described the nonchalance of the ravers' sexual exploits, dancing and drug taking as bluntly as he did. Anton's hero is called Tom, who's permanently doped up on schnaps-drenched muesli and acid sausage. The absolute cliché of a raver, Tom is always on the lookout for even more sex, more drugs. 'Tom's cock hurts like fuck. Finally kaput, it seems.' Schooled in the serial excesses of de Sade, the psychedelic gonzo journalism of Hunter S. Thompson and tongue-in-cheek 1970s German porno voice-overs, Anton exaggerated what went on in the clubs.

The years after 1989 were a party whose intensity occasionally dipped due to fatigue, but basically never stopped. Even today, Berlin's party culture is still marked by a desire to extend for as long as possible a euphoric state where everyday rules are waived. Many people regard the Berghain as the best club in the world, an Olympus of hedonism where the party starts on Saturday evening and goes on till Monday morning. The walls of the old power station enclose an extraterritorial zone where the rave culture of Mitte lives on. Here, the flame lit in the year after the fall of the Wall is passed to tourists from all over the world.

Back in the nineties, the partying was in the heart of the city, both an element, and the expression, of a profound upheaval. Nowadays, it obeys the rules of the entertainment industry: for one night, you check out of a daily grind that has long since reclaimed its dues. Nowadays, no one sits outside the Friscur, a hundred metres from Stadtmitte station, strafing the streets of Mitte with sound.

There is no record of the twenty-four-hour party in the
summer of 1995.

'Of course there isn't!', Anton Waldt says. 'We always
planned to record the live sets, especially because they
weren't made up of ready-made sections. And we were notorious for mucking it up. In hindsight, it's all for the best, all
part of the same vanishing act as the Friseur did.'

Partying comes and goes. It can't be captured – or only in
stories.

Two days before Krautok starts that Friday, the bulldozer
comes back again. The workers came the first time under
cover of darkness. Now, a few hours later, on the morning
of Wednesday 12 July 1995, they're back. At half past nine
Gereon Schmitz rings Daniel Pflumm to announce, 'They're
knocking Mauerstrasse down.'

Daniel grabs his camera and runs over there. He rings the
bell of a flat on the fourth floor of the block of flats opposite,
whose residents have suffered the most from the Elektro's
parties.

'This young lad opened the door. I set up the camera in his
bedroom because they didn't have a balcony, then I cleared
off and only went back to change the tape.'

For three and a half hours Daniel films the demolition of
the building where the Elektro had been until six months
earlier. Later, as he's watching the tape, he discovers that the
kid in whose bedroom his camera was standing was under
house arrest.

'He'd been caught spraying graffiti again. On the video
you can hear his parents giving him a right telling off. They
were shouting and screaming at him, poor guy.'

By the end of the video, all that remains of Mauerstrasse
15 is a few ruined walls and a mountain of rubble. That afternoon, the bulldozer heads home again. The street is shrouded

Fig. 15 Demolition of the building at Mauerstrasse 15, filmed by Daniel Pflumm

in a huge cloud of dust. A police patrol has been there to make sure everything passes off without disturbances. One day is all it takes to destroy the building at Mauerstrasse 15; only months later is the rubble cleared away. The diplomatic centre, the subject of such grand announcements, is never built.

'Dirty tricks were the norm', Daniel Pflumm says. 'There was a committee, and people from the Botschaft took care of that. I thought, "They'd deal with it because of all their contacts. I won't be of much help." I wasn't so happy that they were going over the heads of the squatters, but that lot simply weren't interested. They just wanted to live there. And tomorrow's another day.'

Before the building was cleared, Slavko Stefanoski did the rounds, trying to mobilize people against the eviction and demolition, but there was too great a split between people's activities inside the building.

'There were the occupants, there were the Brazilians and there were the Germans, and the three groups didn't have a lot to do with one another. We never really formed a community. If we'd had a common project, all of us together – the Elektro, the Brazilians, me and the others – we might have stood a chance. We were only tolerated for as long as we brought a splash of colour to that bleak area. We fooled around – middle-class kids in the grey city centre. The two of us could have been having this conversation in Mauerstrasse now, smoking a cigarette up on the balcony', says Slavko while he talks to me from an internet café in Ohrid. 'It was nice there. It's a pity it's not there any more.'

One year later the Friseur bade farewell to the area with a week-long party on the vacant plot that now stretched all the way to the WMF building.

'It was the first loss I can remember', says Robert Lippok, a Friseur regular. 'The first time Berlin gobbled up something we really cared about – that corner of Kronenstrasse. When we heard we had to close down and move out . . . It was the first time we had to give something up.'

The crash of 1873

Andreas Muhs headed to Berlin in 1989 to experience the opening of the Wall. He chronicled what he saw in photographs. His pictures show laughing, weeping and beer-swigging Berliners in front of the Wall on 11 November 1989; East Berliners crossing Potsdamer Platz through a wide gap the next day, while West Berlin police officers hold back the crowds for them; East German policemen inspecting the damage caused on the Western side by 'Wall-peckers' with chisels; a street sign that reads 'Berlin' but with the words 'Capital of the GDR' taped over.

Andreas couldn't stop thinking about the city after this experience, and so in the summer of 1991 he moved to Berlin. He became the head of a photo laboratory on Alexanderplatz and carried on taking photos. His camera sought out and recorded the late-nineteenth-century Berlin of empire, industry and imperialism that had subsequently suffered revolution, depression, National Socialism and bombing before being left to rot during the days of the GDR.

Andreas didn't have much time to record this transitional moment. In January 1993 he noted: 'Old East Berlin is shrinking. Yes, fin-de-siècle Berlin is getting smaller and smaller every day. I must select the details that convey the atmosphere more carefully now. There's no longer much point in using a wide-angle lens.'

Renovations were under way, but the main priority was demolition to make room for new developments. High-earning West Germans were seeking to save tax by investing in construction projects, and office blocks were sprouting on vacant sites, some old, some only just cleared by the wrecking ball. The sheer quantity of new office buildings took your breath away.

Journalists often referred to cowboy tactics in their reports on the Berlin property market. Squatters and even regular tenants kept having to ward off raiding parties dispatched to drive out residents. Speculators paid people to smash the pipes and windows in vacant buildings because a previously inhabitable structure could be legally demolished as soon as it had been reduced to a ruin. This was one way round expensive obstacles such as landmark listings, but arson – or 'hot demolition' as it was known – was also occasionally employed. Squatters tried their hardest to preserve the character of these streets, but the old buildings were in the speculators' way.

The old city centre, Friedrichstrasse and Potsdamer Platz witnessed a race to see who could get their major developments up and running first. Investors fought over prime locations. After the fall of the Wall, Hanno Klein, the influential commissioner for investment at the Senate building authority, dreamed of a new Gründerzeit – a new age of founders. Klein ranted and raged against small-minded town planners and architects as well as the 'conservation of social structures', but at the same time he quarrelled with powerful investors and West Berlin's 'concrete mafia'. He was killed by a letter bomb on 12 June 1991; the perpetrator still hasn't been identified.

The real-estate boom of the 1990s bore many similarities to the one a century earlier, whose traces Andreas Muhs sought out in Mitte after the Wall came down. Both the first and the second Gründerzeit began with a reunification. The Prussian victory over France in 1871 federated the many small, autonomous German duchies and principalities into a single state and also filled the new German Empire's coffers with five billion francs in reparations. The Prussian siege of Paris also gave rise to the Commune, during which the state decided to confiscate all vacant apartments. Bismarck deliberately staged Emperor Wilhelm I's coronation at Versailles to humiliate the French, but the Prussians subsequently joined forces with them to crush the Commune. Karl Marx regarded this alliance between victorious and defeated armies against the proletariat as an unprecedented event which represented the 'crumbling into dust' of the old bourgeois society. He wrote,

> The highest heroic effort of which old society is still capable is national war; and this is now proved to be mere governmental humbug, intended to defer the struggle of classes, and to be thrown aside as soon as that class struggle bursts

out into civil war. Class rule is no longer able to disguise itself in a national uniform.[3]

Few people in Berlin showed much interest in the symptoms of a crumbling bourgeois society; they had enough on their plate already.

The great national uprising came, then came war and then came victory. Berlin, the largest city in the newly founded empire, and its clear-sighted inhabitants were immediately conscious of the position in world history that would henceforth be theirs, and the rights and duties that this position entailed. The spirit of entrepreneurship is now spreading its wings,

Felix Philippi wrote in his memoirs, although we will never know if there is not a hint of irony in these words. The reunification of 1871 was the catalyst for Berlin's explosive expansion and rise to a position of being the largest industrial powerhouse on the European continent, all in the space of four decades.

The bourgeois now began to erect imposing buildings in the city centre, and historic structures had to make way. On the subject of this 'work of destruction' targeting what remained of the medieval city, Julius Rodenberg wrote at the end of the nineteenth century that he was finding it hard to recall things he had only recently seen. 'It is all lost and gone; and so short is man's memory that in another ten years we shall read only in books how it used to be here.'

To this day the word 'Gründerzeit' has a nostalgic, somehow old-fashioned and homely ring to it, but it was in fact a

[3] K. Marx and F. Engels, *On the Paris Commune* (Moscow 1971), p. 102.

time of modernization. The large industrial enterprises were consolidated, even the proverbial man in the street had a flutter on the stock market, and the property market boomed.

'It began with speculation on land', wrote Felix Philippi, who was born in Berlin in 1851 and died there seventy years later. In his twenties he watched the bubble begin to inflate.

> It was taken for granted that people would now flock to the imperial capital from the provinces, and this huge purported increase would require thousands of new buildings with ten or twenty thousand new apartments. Berlin was gripped by a construction frenzy. Entire neighbourhoods with endless streets were developed overnight. Those were the days when masons would drive to building sites in the morning in first-class hackney carriages; they could afford to do so.

Investors in office complexes in the 1990s also anticipated a huge increase in companies and people, and construction workers converged on Berlin from every corner of Europe.

Felix Philippi notes that the word 'Gründer' sounded intoxicating when it first came into usage, but was a term of opprobrium by the time the age of the founders was on its way out. When he explains who the founders are and what they sold the public, you are reminded of the inflated promises with which dot-com shares or investments in office buildings were touted in the 1990s.

> These gentlemen's formula was damned simple. They took some industrial establishment or other – let us say a brewery or an engineering works, a developed block of land or a still vacant site – spun a yarn about the absolutely vertiginous future of this company or that to a breathless and attentive

audience in grand-sounding prospectuses that aristocrats were not afraid to endorse (for a fee of course), stirred the pot until it smelled tempting, and then spooned the shares, sugar-coated with the rashest promises and, naturally, generating outrageous profits, down the throats of the avaricious, senseless masses, talked the listed stocks up and up until the entire capital was in private hands, and then slipped their necks out of the noose; only to surprise, dazzle and bamboozle the stupid, naïve and ravenous crowds the next day with prospectuses signed by princes and dukes extolling far more bogus ventures. People 'founded' as if there were no tomorrow.

The project developers floated more and more companies on the stock exchange. Banks with lavish headquarters, mortgage and product companies, railways and wallpaper manufacturers, spinning mills and leatherworks, petroleum refineries and sheet metal plants, steam-powered brick factories, construction firms, building societies and property ... until the bubble burst in the great crash of 1873. Strictly speaking, the Gründerzeit lasted only a few years.

One hundred and twenty years later, construction frenzy hit Berlin again, this time as a result of a special write-off of East German assets. This measure was approved in 1991 as one of a raft of laws designed to halt the rapid disintegration of the East German economy. GDR industry was in a worse state than anticipated. Anyone who felt like saving themselves some taxes started to invest in closed-end funds or loss allocation companies.

The state tried to promote reconstruction in the East with the biggest tax giveaway of all time and ended up increasing the fortunes of savvy Westerners instead. The fatal consequence is that the East has residential estates and palatial office blocks no one needs – and in Bonn there are billion-mark black holes no one controls,

Der Spiegel concluded in 1997.

That year the federal government, the Länder and local authorities estimated that they would collect seventeen billion marks less in taxes, with the tax offices that used to register the highest tax revenues reporting the biggest deficits. It was the wealthy who benefited from the generous write-offs in the East.

The majority of the investments poured into construction projects in eastern Germany. In Berlin-Mitte, one office block after another shot up from the ground, especially in and around Friedrichstrasse. By 1997 the city had 1.3 million square metres of unoccupied office space. Berlin's banks set aside reserves for bad debts; many private individuals had got themselves deep into debt in an attempt to pay less tax and achieve a handsome profit. However, if the offices in the newly built blocks remained vacant for years, the write-down losses turned into real losses. Many tax-savers went bankrupt. And yet the building went on.

Another office block was built on the corner of Kronenstrasse and Mauerstrasse in 1997. It adjoins the WMF building and runs right around the corner where it meets the building at Kronenstrasse 3. Its corner is dramatically curved, as if the building has a secret power of propulsion. The ship has been a popular metaphor with architects in recent decades, presumably because it suggests a global outlook, dynamism and mobility. When it comes to judging this place very close to Friedrichstrasse, you'd be forgiven for thinking that a society's appetite for experimentation is in inverse proportion to the dynamic appearance of its office blocks. Yet perhaps we can expand this observation. This architecture's desire to signal its thrusting dynamism is amplified by the impression that there is a bridge on the roof from which the building can be steered.

This structure now hosts the officers of the KfW banking group, by its own account one of the leading and most experienced development banks in the world. As a bank with no branches and no customer deposits, the KfW refinances its development business exclusively on global capital markets.

The Kreditanstalt für Wiederaufbau [Credit Institute for Reconstruction] was established in 1948 as a public-law legal entity and is now jointly owned by the Federal Republic of Germany and the Bundesländer. It was the occupying British and Americans who ordered the establishment of a central institution to fund post-war reconstruction in their sectors with money from the Marshall Fund.

The fall of the Wall ushered in the Aufbau Ost reconstruction scheme, the largest funding programme in German history. Between the Wende and the mid-nineties, roughly 70 per cent of all domestic economic investment flowed into what are known as the 'new Bundesländer'. By a quirk of history, a branch of the KfW is now based at Mauerstrasse 15 on the very spot where the Brazilian and the Elektro once stood.

6

USP

All things are possible – Berlin is free

Ten days after the Love Parade the president of the United States of America strolls through the Brandenburg Gate with Helmut Kohl, the 'unification chancellor'. Bill Clinton gives his speech 'to the people of Berlin'. In German, Clinton says, 'Nichts wird uns aufhalten. Alles ist möglich. Berlin ist frei' ['Nothing will stop us. All things are possible. Berlin is free']. The transcript reports that at this point there was applause from the people of Berlin before Clinton repeats in English: 'Berlin is free.' Then the US president sets off on a tour of the city with his cavalcade. It is 12 July 1994.

Ritz Mollema says that anyone who wasn't in Mitte after the Wende cannot imagine what it was like. By this he means moments such as when he was sitting on the kerb in Oranienburger Strasse with his friends and Bill Clinton drove past.

'Of course there were security guards on the rooftops, but there we were sitting on the side of the road and who pulled up and wound down his window? Bill Clinton.'

Ritz Mollema is a good-looking guy with laughter lines crisscrossing his face. He was born in Holland and has lived in Berlin most of the time since 1991, always near Tacheles in one of the streets around Oranienburger Tor. Ritz worked as a journalist, a project leader, a hotel manager and a chef on a restaurant ship. Some of his old friends still live in the neighbourhood too. He's pretty glad that things are no longer the way they were. It's easier for him, as a Dutchman, he says, but all the same, this was where the new subcultures of a new Germany emerged after the Wende.

'You can't play that down. It binds me to this area. There were quite a few squats around here in the early nineties. In Tucholskystrasse, Linienstrasse, Auguststrasse, Bergstrasse, in Kleine Hamburger Strasse, and so on', he says. 'And then there were all the Brits and the Irish who were living here because of the construction boom. Buildings were going up like mad, and that's why they brought them over here. There was a sense of community, with an occasional touch of competition, and I was like a go-between for the different groups. I would translate. If things got tense, I would mediate. Everyone knew me, and I wasn't ever really part of any one group.'

After the death of Klaus Fahnert, who'd sat outside Serdar Yildirim's kiosk on his camping chair for ten years, Ritz Mollema started a blog where the bereaved can share their memories.

'I set up the blog pretty quickly with the information I had. I was amazed people found it so fast as not many people knew his surname', Ritz says. 'I knew Klaus well. He was very friendly and open. Kids weren't scared of him and nor were dogs, which is how you can see if they trust someone. Our paths often crossed, and at some stage I supported him. I was able to help him a bit when I lived in Hannoversche Strasse for a while. He could come round for a shower once a week and rest. You weren't doing him any favours by offering him a flat or a room. He felt better out on the street.'

That social environment in which Klaus Fahnert had a roof over his head but could still be free doesn't exist any more.

The attic at Mauerstrasse 15 was probably Klaus Fahnert's last fixed address. When the squatters were forced to move out in winter 1994/5, they were offered flats, but some turned them down. Misha lived for a while in the attic of the house at Kronenstrasse 3, but no one knew where Klaus had gone. A year later he appeared outside Serdar Yildirim's kiosk, which is where Ritz got to know him. From Mauerstrasse you only have to walk a short way to Friedrichstrasse, and from there you keep heading north over the Weidendammer bridge to Oranienburger Tor. Serdar Yildirim's kiosk soon replaced the Elektro and the Friseur in Klaus's life.

One day he returned from Bonn with a broken leg.

'It got infected and looked terrible', Ritz recalls. He accompanied Klaus to the surgery of Jenny De La Torre, who had made it her job to provide first aid and medical treatment to the homeless. Dr De La Torre examined Klaus and diagnosed a risk of thrombosis.

'Winter was coming, and he had to get off the streets or he'd lose his leg', Ritz says.

However, in order to find a place for Klaus to spend the winter, Ritz first had to re-establish his identity. The homeless man had not been officially registered anywhere for decades: in the eyes of the authorities, he no longer existed. Ritz did some research in Klaus Fahnert's home town in

North Rhine Westphalia. After some time, a local official managed to track Klaus down in the records and issued him an identity card.

'So he spent that winter in a homeless hostel in Lehrter Strasse. We would often hang out together during that time. He started to write about his past and his family. What surprised me was how religious he suddenly got. Something came bubbling up inside him.'

Klaus started talking about how he'd been placed in a Catholic institution as a young man.

'He experienced some bad things there. He was there for ages, until he turned twenty-six, as far as I can remember', Ritz says. 'Klaus told me bits and bobs about his life from time to time because we would bump into each other in the street. We'd have a beer together. He was always sitting between the kiosk and the snack stand. I've checked it all in retrospect and realized that everything he told me was true.'

Klaus suffered from schizophrenia. Most of the time it was easy to talk to him, sometimes it wasn't.

'He clammed up towards the end. He'd never get aggressive, but you couldn't get through to him any more. He was very withdrawn in the final year before his death', Ritz says.

After spending the winter in the homeless hostel, Klaus came back to Oranienburger Strasse and could be found sitting on his camping chair next to Serdar's kiosk again.

'He mainly slept in the grounds of Tacheles', Ritz says. 'When the end came, it was sudden. I went to see him, but he wasn't there. I asked where he was. At the kiosk they said they'd taken him to the Charité hospital.'

Serdar's mother was working at the kiosk that day. 'The people from the snack stand found him next to my kiosk at four in the morning. One of them called an ambulance. It came and took him to the Charité. He'd recently been feeling frail. His body couldn't keep up. He didn't want to drink beer any more but vodka instead, to get warm and for the pain', Serdar says.

Klaus Fahnert was taken to the Charité at 3.42 a.m. on 30 November 2005 in an ambulance belonging to the Berlin fire department. After he was given an ECG in accident and emergency and underwent a blood test, the doctors prescribed Klaus beta blockers. Since the night of 1 December was cold (the temperature the next morning was still below zero), he was allowed to stay in hospital.

Later that morning, two officers from the criminal investigations department came to see Serdar Yildirim's mother.

'They asked if we knew Klaus. My mother wanted to know why they were asking', Serdar says. 'They told her he'd died in hospital.'

In fact, Klaus died on a bench outside the Charité. He had lain down there when he came out of A&E that morning. Someone installed a sign outside Serdar's kiosk to announce Klaus's death.

'One of my customers suggested we put out some candles. We did, next to a picture of him. Then some other people bought some vodka and placed a full bottle next to the sign. Lots of people brought something along. After Klaus's death, a few older people wanted to sit down on Klaus's spot, and I said no, even though that place didn't even belong to me. I just didn't want anyone else there.'

A customer comes along, and Serdar serves him casually but affably. He sees a lot of people every night. He's never in his kiosk before ten at night, and sometimes it's even later before he slides into position behind the till.

Tacheles is still there, and the artists are still in the building when Serdar Yildirim sells beer and cigarettes from his container and tells me about Klaus Fahnert. The staircase of Tacheles is still open. Down in the cellar, where Ständige Vertretung used to be, there are puddles of standing water.

The Belarusian artist Alexander Rodin has been turfed out of his studio up in the attic by HSH Nordbank, and Café Zapata and the cinema were reportedly lured out of the building in return for half a million euros. The money came from a lawyer who refused to reveal his client's identity; press reports mention an unnamed investor.

Then one day security guards occupy the entire building and lock the artists out; the idea is to create a fait accompli. A court orders the bank's security people to leave the building, and this is enforced by the police. The Tacheles sponsor organization takes a leaf out of the capitalists' playbook and declares itself bankrupt so that the bank has no one to negotiate with; it now has to get in touch with every single subtenant individually. The bank reconquers the building room by room and applies for an eviction notice against the people using the studio.

There is very little protest in the city against the imminent demise of Tacheles. For tourists it has stood, for many years, as a memorial to the early days of the new Berlin – the equivalent of the Kaiser Wilhelm Memorial Church, but in the east of the city. To Berliners Tacheles is a peculiar vestige of a bygone era. Even Tacheles veterans are ambivalent in their response to the possible end of the project. The never-ending power struggles between the different factions were too bruising, too many residents produced handicrafts for sale and the days when the building used to set the city's cultural agenda are long gone.

Yet even this lament is almost as old as the building itself. As far back as 1992, there were people who thought Tacheles had been hollowed out, with nothing of substance behind the facade. Maybe that is why the building became a symbol of a prehistory too fragmented, too fleeting and too contradictory to be moulded into one grand storyline and become a legend.

Fig. 16 The back of Tacheles, 1991

In the nineties the site was acquired by the Fundus Group, run by the investor Anno August Jagdfeld. It set out a long-term policy ensuring that the listed art house would be used for cultural purposes, and Tacheles was granted a ten-year deal for the symbolic price of one mark. Fundus took out a loan to fund an ambitious project to build business premises and apartment blocks in the heart of Mitte on the empty plot around Tacheles. The company subsequently ran into financial difficulties before the scheme could be realized. The land and the art house were placed in administration, and the receivers were HSH Nordbank, which had had to be rescued from impending ruin during the financial crisis.

After a while the bank cut off the power and water supply to Tacheles. From one day to the next, Serdar Yildirim's container kiosk vanished and with it the photo memorial to Klaus Fahnert. The grounds were fenced off, and on 4 September 2012 the building was definitively cleared.

Our ideals are in ruins, so let's save the ruins, someone wrote on a banner after Tacheles became a squat. You can read it as a perspicacious description of the squatter society, but it can also be understood as a commentary on German history. The plugging of the gaps in the cityscape spelt the end of the post-Wende period; the development of the Tacheles site brought the post-war era in Berlin to a close. The many traces of the city's violent twentieth-century history have themselves been consigned to history.

When the Wall came down, Mitte awoke from a long sleep. The clubs, bars and galleries that sprang up here forged Berlin's image as a wild, creative and productive place. That was only possible because there was available space, and it came about because there were a enough people investing their time, energy and ideas.

There are still enough creative people, and the city is growing. As of 31 December 2019 Berlin had a population of nearly 3.7 million, more than at any time since the end of the war. The city exerts a particular pull on young and creative types from other EU countries. The Senate recognizes the city's colourful and hypercreative scene producing art and music as a unique selling point. However, this culture was only able to flourish after 1989 because space in the city centre was affordable. When a brochure produced by Mitte council's culture department in the early nineties deplored the fact that 'Displacement has already started!', not many people felt particularly concerned, because there was enough room for people to move on when their temporary licence to use premises ran out. Now, though, those possibilities have seriously narrowed. Since reunification the Senate has sold off 85 per cent of public assets in Mitte district, excluding the streets, parks and public facilities, in order to liquidate its interest payments and tempt investors to Berlin. In 2010 the relevant real-estate fund disposed of 533 properties with a total surface area of 1.1 million square metres, including a prison, opera workshops and a day care centre. Of the €190 million of revenue generated by these divestments, €156 million were passed on to the regional treasury, much to the delight of the senators responsible for financial and economic issues.

Twenty-two years after the fall of the Wall, David Bowie released a new single. The track tells the story of a man sitting 'lost in time' in the Dschungel, a legendary disco in the Nürnberger Strasse near the KaDeWe.[1] The narrator recalls twenty thousand people crossing the Böse Bridge – 'fingers are crossed, just in case'. On the western side of the bridge was the Bornholmer Strasse border crossing, which was the first checkpoint to be opened for East German citizens to walk through on the evening of 9 November. The song's chorus asks, 'Where are we now?' David Bowie appears to feel that the fall of the Wall was a once-in-a-generation event whose memory he associates with a sense of loss.

Most people who were out and about in Mitte after the fall of the Wall speak about the past with a cheerful, composed awareness that they possess something that can never be taken away from them. They enjoyed the possibility of being able to move with others to a beat of their own defining without having to analyse its meaning and purpose. That may be the reason why not everyone wants to disclose everything. The most telling words are usually spoken only when the tape has stopped recording – or not at all. People prefer to keep certain experiences to themselves. Their unease about the historicizing, defining and archiving of their

---

[1] KaDeWe, or Kaufhaus des Westens ('Department Store of the West'), was founded in 1907 and is the largest department store in Europe after Harrods.

experiences doesn't only stem from a recognition that the magic of particular moments lies in the fact that they are unrepeatable; it is also linked to a suspicion that historicization cuts us off from our own experiences. Those parties in Mitte may have been the last opportunity to do something that was not simultaneously posted online, recorded and marked in the correct place on your timeline. What might seem like repressing memories is actually the need to keep the flame alive, sustain the inner connection, hold onto the moment. The refusal to be photographed indulging in your night-time rituals has similarities to a refusal to shed experiences, emotions and ideas by speaking about them.

One of the most beautiful gestures of this period relates to the futility of trying to represent certain experiences. The New Yorker Elizabeth Felicella, who came to Berlin to study, photobombed tourists snapping themselves in front of the Brandenburg Gate. No traceable evidence of this work remains. The photos featuring Elizabeth Felicella alongside tourists in front of the Brandenburg Gate are now found in photo albums slumbering in drawers in living rooms all over the world. Some day, when those tourists' children and grandchildren look at those pictures, they may wonder about the identity of this smiling stranger who has smuggled her way into the frame.

Christoph Keller's final bar shift at the Friseur was on 5 July 1996, shortly before the place closed its doors for ever. It was a Friday. Christoph is sure of that because that evening he breached the ban on photography and positioned his video camera on one of the shelves behind him, between the gin and the whisky. Its incorruptible eye stared over his shoulder for several hours, recording who ordered drinks, who sat down on the bar stools, who spoke to their neighbours and who ignored the person next to them. The quality of the recording is poor; it's too dark inside the Friseur to make out faces, and time has taken its toll on the VHS copy.

'You're on there too', Christoph says. We forward-wind the tape at random and press play. Someone comes up to the left-hand side of the bar, orders and is handed a beer. By his silver-framed glasses and his movements, I recognize the man I must have been.

Bibliography

Adilkno, *Cracking the Movement*, New York 1994.

Agentur Bilwet, *Bewegungslehre: Botschaften aus einer autonomen Wirklichkeit* [*Movement Teachings: Messages from an Autonomous Reality* – untranslated], Berlin and Amsterdam, 1991.

'Anarchie ist Arbeit', *Der Spiegel* (1990), No. 32.

Baum, K.-H., 'Fliegende Urnen und der Schwund der Gegenstimmen', *Frankfurter Rundschau*, 9 May 1989.

'Berichte über die Luftangriffe auf die Reichshauptstadt', Hauptluftschutzstelle in Berlin. Landesarchiv Berlin. A Rep. 001-02, No. 701–708, Film A 4818; A Rep. 005-07, No. 558.

Bey, H., *T.A.Z.: The Temporary Autonomous Zone: Ontological Anarchy, Poetic Terrorism*, 2nd edn, Brooklyn 2003.

Biddle, T. D., 'Wartime Reactions', in P. Addison and J. A. Crang (eds.), *Firestorm: The Bombing of Dresden 1945*, London 2006.

Bittner, A., Jungbluth, R. and Schäfer, U., 'Fehl-Steuer Ost', *Der Spiegel* (1997), No. 46.

Böhm, A., 'Wie in einem "okkupierten Land"', *die tageszeitung*, 15 Nov. 1990.

Clewing, U., 'Mäusegang durch fünf Kontinente', *die tageszeitung*, 31 Aug. 1991.

DJ, 'Tod vor der Rettungsstelle', *Berliner Woche*, 22 Mar. 2006.

Fest, J., *Inside Hitler's Bunker: The Last Days of the Third Reich*, London 2005.

Frankenthal, H., *Verweigerte Rückkehr: Erfahrungen nach dem Judenmord* [*Refused Return: Experiences after the Holocaust* – untranslated], Frankfurt am Main 1999.

Geisel, E., *Die Banalität der Guten: Deutsche Seelenwanderungen* [*The Banality of the Good: Wandering German Souls* – untranslated], Berlin 1992.

Geisel, E., *Im Scheunenviertel* [*In the Barn Quarter* – untranslated], foreword G. Kunert, Berlin 1981.

Geist, J. F. and Kürvers, K., *Das Berliner Mietshaus 1740–1862* [*The Tenements of Berlin 1740–1862* – untranslated], Munich 1980.

Heller, L., 'Linienstrasse', in H. Knobloch, *Der Berliner zweifelt immer* [*A Berliner Always Doubts* – untranslated], Berlin 1986.

Hoppe, R., 'Der Rosenthaler Platz unterhält sich', http://www.berlinstreet.de/4432

Hwang, Sung-Uk Brad, 'Gespensteruntersuchung', http://de.scribd.com/doc/52505719/Gespensteruntersuchung

John, T., 'Zukunft eimerweise. 11 Jahre Kulturhaus "I.M. Eimer"', *Scheinschlag* (2001), No. 1.

Kaiser, A., 'Geschmack der Elendsviertel mitten in der Hauptstadt', *die tageszeitung*, 30 May 1991.

Kellermann, E., 'Die verdrängte Nazi-Ungeist in der DDR', *Freies Wort*, 16 July 2007.

Knobloch, H., *Stadtmitte umsteigen* [*Change at Stadtmitte* – untranslated], Berlin 1982.

Kugler, A., 'Oben wumm! Und unten klatsch!', *die tageszeitung*, 30 May 1994.

Kuhlbrodt, D., 'Je älter, desto früher', *die tageszeitung*, 25 Feb. 2012.

Kuhlbrodt, D., 'Stadt der verlorenen Seelen: Berlin Blues', in R. von Praunheim, 'Film' No. 30, Munich 1983.

Kuhrt, A., 'Der Naziüberfall auf die Zionskirche', http://www.berlinstreet.de/4432

Lachenicht, G., 'Getauft und deportiert', *Jahrbuch für Berlin-Brandenburgische Kirchengeschichte* (2007), No. 66.

Leinemann, J., 'Ein Herz und eine Mitte', *Der Spiegel* (1991), No. 19.

Liebmann, I., *Stille Mitte von Berlin* [*Mitte: The Silent Centre of Berlin* – untranslated], Berlin 2002.

'Liste der vom Abriss bedrohten Häuser in Berlin-Mitte', *die tageszeitung*, 9 Jul. 1994.

Maier, A., 'Die Nacht der Nazis in der Zionskirche', *die tageszeitung*, 27 Sep. 2008.

Marx, K. and Engels, F., *On the Paris Commune*, Moscow 1971.

Muhs, A., *Berlin: Die frühen Neunziger. Fotografien 1989–1994*, Leipzig 2010.

Nafziger, J., 'Obdachlose haben meist eine andere Wahl', *tagesschau.de*, 19 Sep. 2002.

Noll, C., *Der goldene Löffel* [*The Golden Spoon* – untranslated], Stuttgart 1989.

O'Donnell, J. P. and Bahnsen, U., *The Bunker: The History of the Reich Chancellery Group*, New York 1978.

Philippi, F., 'Die Gründerzeit', in H. Knobloch, *Der Berliner zweifelt immer* [*A Berliner Always Doubts* – untranslated], Berlin 1986.

Preuss, U. K., 'Der Liquidationsvertrag', *die tageszeitung*, 14 Sep. 1990.

Rada, U., 'Baustadträte solidarisch mit Dubrau', *die tageszeitung*, 2 Jun. 1995.

Rada, U., 'Das Ende der Anarchie', *die tageszeitung*, 13 Nov. 2010.

Rada, U., 'Die Räumung war schon vorher absehbar', interview with Bernd Finger, *die tageszeitung*, 16 Nov. 2010.

Rodenberg, J., 'Das Herz von Berlin', in H. Knobloch,

Der Berliner zweifelt immer [*A Berliner Always Doubts* – untranslated], Berlin 1986.

Rodenberg, J., 'Der Norden Berlins', in H. Knobloch, *Der Berliner zweifelt immer* [*A Berliner Always Doubts* – untranslated], Berlin 1986.

Sadr-Haghighian, N., 'What's the Time, Mahagonny?', *e-flux journal* (2010), No. 17.

Siedler, W. J., 'Stadt als Landschaft', *Berliner Zeitung*, 21 Feb. 1998.

Steglich, U. and Kratz, P., *Das falsche Scheunenviertel: Ein Vorstadtverführer* [*The Other Scheunenviertel: A Misguidebook to the Vorstadt* - untranslated], Berlin 1993.

Waldt, A., *Auf die zwölf* [*Smack in the Face* – untranslated], Berlin 2010.

Weber, A., 'Mo wie Minimalismus', *die tageszeitung*, 19 Nov. 1994.

Willems, S., *Der entsiedelte Jude: Albert Speers Wohnungsmarktpolitik für den Berliner Hauptstadtbau* [*Deporting the Jews: Albert Speer's Housing Market Policy and Making Berlin the Capital of the Reich* – untranslated], Berlin 2002.

Winkler, T., 'Im grauen Osten blühte er', *die tageszeitung*, 13 Dec. 2000.